There could scarcely be a mo[re] and helpful book than this for c[...] ministries to center upon God's ~~rd. Here is a primer on bibliology, hermeneutics, and pedagogy that does not mention the words! Youth ministers and those who work with students will be profoundly instructed on what the Bible is, how it works, and how to teach it. And more, they will learn from a youth pastor who has done it and continues to do it amid the swirling idioms of popular culture.

—**R. Kent Hughes,** Senior Pastor Emeritus of College Church in Wheaton, Illinois

Bible Study is a must read for the next generation looking to make a difference for God. With tools to read and understand God's Word, Jon Nielson ultimately trains us for usefulness in God's world. This book is clear, accessible, and written by a leader with a passion for gospel growth. So get it, read it, and then go for it.

—**David Helm,** Pastor of Holy Trinity Church in Chicago; Executive Director of Charles Simeon Trust

Jon Nielson rightly believes that even students are able to understand Scripture at the highest level. This volume is an engaging expression of that belief, helpful for Christian young people as well as those who lead them.

—**Randall J. Gruendyke,** Campus Pastor at Taylor University

If you want your ministry to be healthy, God-centered, and gospel-driven, then there is only one way to do it: make the Bible its life blood. Make the study of the text, obedience to the text, and the God of the text the centerpiece of everything you do. As a former leader in my ministry at College Church and now the pastor of that very ministry, I could not be prouder of Jon. This book reflects the Bibline culture both of us were raised with as young leaders at a church where we saw the inestimable fruits of a Word-driven ministry.

—**Jay Thomas,** Lead Pastor of Chapel Hill Bible Church in Chapel Hill, North Carolina

Imagine this: teenagers getting excited about hearing God speak through his Word. Add to that those same young people learning how to read and study God's Word better, with a growing understanding of such things as biblical theology and genre and how to lead a small group. If you're excited about this prospect, read this book. You will not be disappointed!

—**Jenny Salt,** Dean of Students at Sydney Missionary and Bible College in Sydney, Australia

Jon Nielson has put together a compelling and clear guide to embedding Bible study in youth group ministries.

—**Josh Moody,** Senior Pastor of College Church in Wheaton

BIBLE STUDY

BIBLE STUDY

A STUDENT'S GUIDE

JON NIELSON

P.O. BOX 817 • PHILLIPSBURG • NEW JERSEY 08865-0817

ISBN: 978-1-59638-637-2 (pbk)
ISBN: 978-1-59638-638-9 (ePub)
ISBN: 978-1-59638-639-6 (Mobi)

Printed in the United States of America

I dedicate this book to Jeanne—
my wife, and my best friend.

CONTENTS

FOREWORD

D. A. Carson

READERS HAVE LONG OBSERVED that the best children's books are those that adults enjoy no less than their children do. Are the Chronicles of Narnia to be cherished only by children under the age of ten? Of course, adults may appreciate the books for reasons that in part entirely escape the notice of their children. But the best children's literature transcends categorization by age.

Although it is a very different genre, the book you are holding in your hand, designed to help high schoolers engage in enjoyable and careful Bible study, will doubtless prove to be a considerable help to older readers as well. That is because Jon Nielson takes his primary readers seriously. Though the book is written with a light touch and with plenty of deft, age-suitable illustrations, it expects high schoolers to think seriously about their faith. The Bible, Jon says, is God speaking; it is powerful; it is understandable; it is a literary product; it is one story. Theologians will recognize that behind these formulas lie an array of hugely complex and important notions, and Jon teases them out: he makes them clear, and he shows what relevance they have for Bible study—whether Bible study undertaken by a sixteen-year-old or a fifty-year-old. For every age group must be reminded that God holds in honor those who are humble and contrite and who tremble at his Word. Driving home this lesson *before* outlining some "how to's" is what makes this book eminently helpful.

So if you are a high schooler, read this book carefully and thoughtfully, and then loan it to your parents. Chances are pretty good that they'll benefit from it as much as you will. If you are a parent of high schoolers, or concerned for the welfare of high schoolers you know who are not your own children, put a copy of this book into their hands and encourage them to read it. Better yet, work through it with them, or at very least read it before you give it away. They won't mind, especially if you tell them that the reason you are giving this book to them is because you have found it so helpful yourself.

ACKNOWLEDGMENTS

THIS BOOK CAME INTO BEING, in large part, due to the careful and diligent life work of my mother, Kathleen Nielson. For as long as I can remember, she has given herself to what I believe she sees as her greatest calling: studying God's Word and helping others, specifically women, do the same. Her passionate pursuit of understanding God's Word, loving it, and communicating it to others has long been a shining example to me. Last year, she articulated her basic mind-set and approach to Bible study in her book *Bible Study: Following the Ways of the Word*. It was this book that led to the writing of the book you're about to read. It was her desire—and the desire of the P&R team—to put some of the same concepts into slightly different packaging for young people in Christian churches around the world. I certainly hope I've done justice to this "youth version" of her book!

I'd like to thank the helpful people at P&R for working with me on this project. I appreciate their confidence, diligence, and partnership. I'm thankful, too, that they believe in the importance of helping people in the church today—especially young people—study the Scriptures in order to grow in grace, knowledge, and holiness, to the glory of our Lord and Savior Jesus Christ!

College Church in Wheaton, Illinois, has been—for the past three years—the central place for my ministry, leadership, and shepherding. I am grateful for the godly families in our

11

church, who have raised their children to love God's Word and worship Jesus Christ. In youth ministry, and now in college ministry, I have so often had the benefit of simply building on already existing foundations. Jeanne and I praise God for this rich season of ministry in Wheaton, and we thank Jesus for the gospel work and gospel growth that is happening in this local church.

My wife, Jeanne, has been a constant support and encouragement to me; I thank God for her, and I am grateful for her love and faithfulness to me. Our daughters, too—Adelyn and Averie—have given me some inspiration as well. They're still young! But I hope and pray that they will grow up studying, loving, and speaking God's Word as they embrace Jesus Christ as their Lord and Savior.

INTRODUCTION

"Many teenagers know abundant details about the lives of favorite musicians and television stars or about what it takes to get into a good college, but most are not very clear on who Moses and Jesus were."
—CHRISTIAN SMITH and
MELINDA LUNDQUIST DENTON [1]

SIX STUDENTS SIT TOGETHER in a family room, somewhere in the Midwest. They're doing a Bible study together. Ben, the discussion leader, asks the guys and girls to open their Bibles to Philippians 4:10–13, their passage for the evening. As they settle into the couches and chairs on which they are sitting, Kristen reads the passage out loud:

> I rejoiced in the Lord greatly that now at length you have revived your concern for me. You were indeed concerned for me, but you had no opportunity. Not that I am speaking of being in need, for I have learned in whatever situation I am to be content. I know how to be brought low, and I know how to abound. In any and every circumstance, I have learned the secret of facing plenty and hunger, abundance and need. I can do all things through him who strengthens me.

Ben asks, "So, what is this passage saying to us?" Michael, a football player at a Christian school, jumps in right away:

"I love that last verse. It's on the wall in the weight room at school—really inspiring for me when I'm working out!" Hannah speaks up: "Yeah, it's so cool. It seems like it's saying that we can really, like, just do anything with Jesus on our side." This reminds Ben of a recent test he took, for which he hadn't studied very hard. He had prayed for success, and was able to get a good grade after all; he tells the story to the group. The conversation continues, and before they know it, the "Bible study" has ended and it's time to go home. Kevin, who hasn't said much, walks to his car wondering what the apostle Paul really meant when he wrote those words to the Philippians so many years ago . . .

Have you been there? I have. Probably all of us who have been in the church for a while have been a part of a "Bible study" that didn't turn out to have much "Bible" or "study" about it at all. Too often, these gatherings end up being times for sharing feelings, thoughts, or concerns, or even valuable times of Christian fellowship and mutual encouragement. But what is Bible study, really? Can we attach this title to any gathering at which people open up a Bible at some point, even if they only use it to launch into an unrelated conversation? Some of you might be wondering whether real Bible study can actually be fun and interesting. Can it work for students today?

> "One big problem with youth Bible study is the propensity of teen studies to treat the Bible like an answer book for problems, both moral and emotional, rather than as a narrative of God's redemptive work. Often the big idea is to obey God, but without God as the big idea, that is pretty lame."
>
> —Barnabas Piper (former youth leader, College Church in Wheaton, Illinois)

I think we can probably all agree that there is, today, a real need to clarify what it means to study the Bible. There is a place for prayer groups—they are wonderful! There is a place for groups of students who get together for the purpose of confession and accountability—that is much needed! It is even helpful for Christian teenagers to gather for the sole purpose of sharing struggles with each other as they seek to live for Christ in schools and communities filled with sin and brokenness. But there is a place—a too-often-vacant place—for Bible study as well. Christian teenagers need to be digging into God's Word in a real way. Gospel-centered students need to rediscover real Bible study, for the good of their hearts and souls.

But providing a definition of Bible study will not be enough to make this happen. Young people need to be trained and taught how to *actually do it*. Students who are convinced that Bible study is necessary, and even understand what Bible study is, may still lack the "tools" to actually study the Bible on their own, much less lead their peers into a meaningful engagement with Scripture. We need to rediscover what Bible study is, *and* we need to figure out how to train young people to do it.

This is true, most basically, because of what the Bible is: God's inspired Word, given to the people he created. We can't know God apart from his Word! If this is really true, then the dynamic described by Christian Smith and Melinda Lundquist Denton in the quotation that began this introduction is a tragedy. Young people today need to know the Bible. They need to hear God's Word, and all that it has to say to them about creation, sin, and salvation in Jesus Christ. The best way for them to get there is by learning how to *study* the Bible!

If you're a teenager and you love Jesus, this book is for you. If you work with teenage students, this book is for you. If you're the parent of a teenager, I pray that this book is encouraging and helpful to you as well.

This book is grounded in five main theological truths about the Bible. We'll look at these five truths in turn:

1. The Bible is *God speaking*: the "inspiration" of the Bible
2. The Bible is *powerful*: the "authority" of the Bible
3. The Bible is *understandable*: the "perspicuity" of the Bible
4. The Bible is *literary*: the "nature" of the Bible as literature
5. The Bible is *one story*: the "unity" of the Bible, with one main author

My goal is to take these basic truths about the Bible and show how they apply to Bible study—both to what it is and to how we should do it. We'll take some "big-picture" looks at the theology of the Bible, but we'll get very practical, too, by the end of the book.

Along the way, you'll be exposed to a lot of stories and quotations from real students and youth leaders who have gotten excited about real Bible study, and have also faced the real challenges and struggles connected with making Bible study "work" for young people. I hope these are very encouraging and enlightening to you; they certainly have been to me!

Before we get into it, let me just attest that I am not an expert at this! I began writing this book during my time as a high school pastor at College Church in Wheaton, Illinois. Now, as a college pastor at the same church, I'm still learning every day how to help the students I lead study the Bible in the best way possible. We're still figuring it out! But my core conviction is that God—the mighty Creator God of the universe—speaks to young people (and old people) most fundamentally through his Word. If that's true, then we need to figure out how to study his Word better. We want to hear God speak. There is no voice more important for students to hear.

1

THE BIBLE IS
GOD SPEAKING

"If it is true that the Bible tells us about God, not least
what kind of God he is, it is no less true that unless God
really is that sort of God, it is impossible to appreciate
the Bible for what it is. To approach the Bible correctly
it is important to know something of the God who stands
behind it."

—D. A. CARSON[1]

HAVE YOU BEEN THERE?

Ryan had heard it since he was a little kid. "The Bible is
the inspired Word of God." It had never meant very much to
him—an answer to a theological trivia question in Sunday
school, nothing more. After all, we refer to lots of things as
"inspired," right? We talk about artists who have a moment of
inspiration, and then go on to create beautiful works of art.
Athletes, after a great game, have been known to say things like

17

this: "I was just really inspired by what Coach said to the team at halftime in the locker room." Ryan had always had a vague impression that the inspiration of the Bible must be slightly different from what happens to an artist or an athlete, but he wasn't quite sure how to work it out. Did it mean that the Bible is special in some way? Did it mean that God made the Bible magically appear? Could it really mean that God still speaks to people today through a several-thousand-year-old book?

INSPIRATION

The Bible. Sixty-six books. Forty different authors. Around 1,500 years in production. And this is all together in one volume. Kind of amazing, isn't it? Some of these facts have served as bases for many attacks on the Bible and its reliability. How can we really believe that all those different authors—over more than a thousand years—could put together something that has any relevance for us today? The simple answer is this: God is the author of the Bible. Yes, there are human authors who composed the books of the Bible, but there is ultimately one main author: God.

We can say that God is the author of the Bible because of the Christian doctrine of *inspiration*. This doctrine teaches that the human authors of the Bible were inspired by God the Holy Spirit to write exactly the words that God intended them to write. In Scripture, the word "inspiration" communicates the sense that these human authors were "carried along" by the Holy Spirit as they wrote (2 Peter 1:21), and that the Holy Spirit "breathed" into them in a way that ensured that their words would be God's words. Because of inspiration, we can say that God is the author of the Bible. The Bible is God speaking.

Listen to the way the apostle Paul summarizes the biblical truth of inspiration: "All Scripture is breathed out by God and profitable for teaching, for reproof, for correction, and for training in righteousness" (2 Tim. 3:16). He makes a really incredible statement, doesn't he? All Scripture—all the books written by various human authors over hundreds of years—is "breathed out" by God. That is what the Bible teaches. Now, let's not get inspiration mixed up with dictation. Some of you may have a picture in your minds of God somehow taking control of Moses' arm and guiding every stroke of his pen by force while Moses took a nap. That is not what we're talking about here! The human authors wrote from their own experience, personalities, and situations—as we'll see later in this book when we talk about literary genres. But God in his power and wisdom guided their writing perfectly and carefully so as to lead them to include exactly what he wanted in the book that would guide his people for the rest of human history. His leading was sure, intentional, and perfect, even while they wrote out of their unique personalities and situations. That is an amazing work of an incredibly wise and powerful God, and it makes Scripture absolutely unique; there is no book like it in the world, and there never will be!

AN ILLUSTRATION OF INSPIRATION

I have a wonderful assistant who helps me in many ways with the youth and student ministry at our church. Sometimes I ask her to do things. (OK, I ask her to do things a lot!) Let's say that I ask her to make a reservation for our youth group at a camp. I might call her on the phone to ask her to do that. I might walk over to her desk and ask her in person. I might send her an e-mail. Now, let's say I choose the last option: I send her an e-mail, asking her to make a reservation at a camp. Then, a couple of days later, I ask her whether she's made the reservation, and she says, "No, of course not. All I got was an e-mail from you." Would that be right? No, of course not. Why? Because, for my assistant, an e-mail instruction is as good as a face-to-face instruction. This sounds weird, but where my e-mail speaks, I speak! That is what we are saying about the Bible. Where the Bible speaks, God speaks. Period. So, what does that mean for how we view the Bible?

IMPLICATIONS FOR HOW WE SEE THE BIBLE

If this fundamental truth of inspiration is indeed a truth, then we need to affirm that *everything* in the Bible is true. God doesn't mess up. In other words, we can read any passage in the Bible and know that it is accurate and correct in what it portrays. The Bible is reliable. This belief does call for a certain amount of faith. We are called to believe in a God who is powerful enough to carefully oversee the writing of thousands and thousands of words—using human authors to accomplish his great purpose of communication with the people he created.

There is another fundamental truth that comes from the doctrine of inspiration, or the idea that the Bible is God speaking. This is the truth of "authorial intent." In other words, if God is the author of the Bible, then the Bible *means* something. And its ultimate meaning is what God—the author—*intended* it to mean. This concept is going to fly in the face of a lot of what you are probably being taught in your literature classes today. Some of you have heard of "reader response theory," the idea that the reader of a text is the one who really determines what the text means. That concept has worked its way into a lot of Bible studies. You'll know that this idea is at play when you hear someone ask the question, "What does this Bible passage mean *to you*?" Now, that's not always a bad question, but it should never be the *first* question that we ask in Bible study. Because the Bible is God speaking—because God is the ultimate author of the Bible—the first question we should always ask is, "What does this Bible passage mean—and what does God intend it to mean?" Because God is the author of the Bible, and because he does intend the words to mean something specific, that question is answerable for us in the context of Bible study, although it may require hard work!

Another way to communicate this idea is through this important statement about Scripture: "The Bible can't mean something that it *never* meant." The Bible's meaning doesn't change based on time, audience, or situation. It meant something to its original audience, and that original meaning still guides how we interpret the Bible today. The Bible teaches "timeless theological truths"—realities about God that will never change, even while they are grounded in the historical events and situations of the human biblical authors. The God we hear from today, through Scripture, is the same God who spoke to and led his people so many years ago.

That leads us to a third implication of the doctrine of inspiration. If the Bible is God speaking, then everything in the Bible is there *on purpose*. I'm sure some of you have at some point in your lives (maybe in the midst of getting bogged down in the book of Leviticus in your personal devotions) wondered whether parts of the Bible just "slipped through the cracks." Did God really mean for this passage to be in the Bible? Is this really important? What we are saying, when we affirm that the Bible is God speaking, is that the *entire* Bible is God speaking. It's all there on purpose, for our benefit, and according to the will of God. It is all, therefore, worth reading, studying, and understanding. God, the ultimate author of Scripture, put the Bible together in a purposeful way.

Finally, if the Bible is God speaking, then we need to realize that the Bible is *still speaking today*. The doctrine of inspiration leads us to see the Bible as completely different from any other book in the entire world. It is alive! We can actually hear God's voice in the words of the Bible. Scripture has the ability to touch us and affect us in powerful ways—in ways that no other book can. Listen to how the author of Hebrews describes the living nature of Scripture: "For the word of God is living and active, sharper than any two-edged sword, piercing to the division of soul and of spirit, of joints and of marrow, and discerning the thoughts and intentions of the heart" (Heb. 4:12). This is no ordinary book. The Bible is God speaking. And God—the living God of the universe—still speaks powerfully through his written Word today.

So, before we get into some implications of inspiration for Bible study, let's summarize what we've been saying here. God is the author of the Bible; the Bible is therefore God speaking. We can even say this in a slightly stronger way: where the Bible speaks, God speaks. This means that the Bible is true. It has a discernible meaning (based on its author's intent). It is intentionally put together by God. And it is still alive and powerful, since God is still speaking through it to his people today.

IMPLICATIONS FOR HOW WE STUDY THE BIBLE

The Nature of Bible Study: It Is Personal

A lot of you have been to a lot of Bible studies. Some of you have not enjoyed them. You can be honest if that's you! That's been me at many points. Bible studies can be dry, formal, even boring. Sometimes, I think, that's what drives students away from real Bible study toward meetings that are a little more focused on fellowship, sharing, and accountability. But could it be that we are reacting against—not Bible study itself—but a certain *nature* of some Bible studies?

Bible studies that are boring have missed an important point. Because of the doctrine of inspiration that we've just been talking about (the fact that the Bible is God speaking), Bible studies should be fundamentally *personal* even more than they are *propositional*. That's a fancy way to say that Bible studies shouldn't be just about getting through a set of questions, or learning some facts about a passage. They should be about personally engaging the God who talks to us through his Word! Bible studies that stop at propositions and don't move people closer to the personal God of the universe have completely missed their point.

Imagine, for example, that a girl or guy you really like at school writes you a letter. You stuff it in your pocket during class, and save it to read later when you're safely in your room. Finally the day is over, and you rush home, close the door to your room, and unfold the letter. Imagine reading that letter and just focusing on the facts in an "academic" way. "OK," you say to yourself, "this is a letter from my crush to me, focusing on this person's romantic interest in me and admiration for some specific qualities about my personality and appearance." I don't think so. You're going to *pore* over that letter, aren't you? You're going to analyze every line—not just to get the facts, but to feel the meaning and the emotion behind the words. You're going to let the words affect you personally; you understand that the letter is coming from the hands of a person you're crazy about. There is nothing boring about reading that letter!

That's how our Bible study should be. We don't come together around God's Word to get a list of facts or a stale summary of a passage. We come together around God's Word to let the *personal* God of the universe speak *personally* into our lives. Bible study should be intensely personal, because we know that a person—God himself—is behind the words that we read and study together. And the only way this can happen is if we are first part of the community of God. The Bible speaks to us personally as we are corporately invested in Christ's community, the church. That will be part of my argument for why Bible study is so important!

> "Going to church, listening to sermons, singing songs in worship, and personal Bible reading were all very formative and important to me, but in a student Bible study (particularly *student-led* Bible studies), I often had trouble seeing their worth. As a rather introverted person, hanging out with people was always a sort of a struggle, but finding value in *discussion* about the Bible was also difficult. What could a group of high schoolers possibly discover in this text that would not only overcome the awkwardness of learning how to discuss ideas/topics/themes but would also be personal enough to allow us to be vulnerable and to apply the Scripture to our lives?"
>
> —Mike Solis (student, Wheaton College in Wheaton, Illinois)

We do need to clarify this a little bit and note that by *personal* we do not mean "relative." In other words, the personal nature of Bible study does not take away the reality of authorial intent—that a Bible passage does have a meaning that is determined by its author, and ultimately the God who inspired the human author. "Personal" Bible study does not mean Bible study that turns directly to individual experience, asking only, "What does this mean to me?" The personal nature comes *through* the discovery of the true meaning of Scripture. Personal Bible study is discovering, in the context of Bible study, the meaning of a Bible passage, and then allowing that truth to speak directly to your own mind, heart, and life. It is a commitment to not stop at academic discovery, but to continue into personal application and reception. It is finding the truths of the Scripture and letting them change your life.

To illustrate this, let's go back to the story of the love letter from your crush. The personal nature of that letter doesn't mean that you make that letter mean whatever you want it to mean! In fact, if you really care about this person, your goal in reading it will be to figure out *exactly* what that letter means. What does your crush mean by "interested"? What was the intention behind that scary word, "unsure"? If anything, the personal nature of a love letter makes you even more determined to understand the intended meaning absolutely correctly.

THE HOLY SPIRIT'S ROLE IN BIBLE STUDY

All this discussion about the personal nature of Bible study points us to the fact that this is not a dead exercise. A Bible study is not like a book club, which is made up of a group of humans alone, discussing a book written by a human author. Bible study is not dead because the Holy Spirit—the third person of the Trinity—is intimately involved. That is the wonder, and the supernatural nature, of a true Bible study. It is a group of humans, yes, but as they dig into God's inspired Word, the Holy Spirit is active, making the Word do its work of confrontation, conviction, and application. Bible study is a supernatural, "living" kind of exercise, because the Holy Spirit is intimately involved in it.

We can't miss this! The reason that studying the Bible is different from studying any other book is that the Bible was composed by human authors who were *inspired by the Holy Spirit*. The reason that studying the Bible today is really about hearing God's voice is that *the Holy Spirit still speaks to people today through the Bible.* This means that, when we correctly interpret what the Bible is saying, we participate in allowing the opportunity for God's Holy Spirit to communicate to people in a powerful, true, real, and relevant way. It is so important for us to understand the study of the Bible this way. We need to "get it right," because only then can we understand the Holy Spirit in the way he speaks to God's people!

The Goal of Bible Study: To Hear God Speak

You can see that we're definitely approaching the final goal of Bible study. If the Bible is God speaking, then the goal of Bible study, ultimately, is to hear God speak as clearly as possible. It is not just to get the right answers or to learn things that are true. The goal of Bible study should ultimately be hearing God talk to us through his written and inspired Word, by the power of his Holy Spirit, who is actively working through the Bible.

Let's go back to the story about the love letter from your crush at school. We pointed out already that you wouldn't read that letter just to get propositional truths out of it, or in order to put together a concise summary of its content. You would read it personally, conscious of the fact that it was written to you by a special person. But the personal aspect of that letter would not mean you would read it any less carefully. If anything, it would cause you to read it *more* carefully! You wouldn't want to miss a single word. You'd probably read it a few times, just to make sure you had grasped the main point, and really understood what it was saying. The personal nature of that letter would cause you to give great concentration to getting it right, so that you could accurately understand what that person was trying to communicate to you.

This idea can be applied to Bible study as well. A group of students studying the Bible together should be very focused on "getting it right." They should be absolutely sure that they've made their way to the main point of a passage. But this isn't so they can get a grade, pass a test, or check a box that says "Bible study: Completed." They should do those things in a Bible study—work hard to get it right, find the main point, discover the right application—so that they can hear God speak to them clearly and personally through his inspired written Word. And that is never boring.

We cannot overemphasize the importance of "getting it right" in a Bible study. If the goal of Bible study is to hear God speak, then we should be doing everything we can to correctly understand any passage in the Bible so that we don't *think* we hear God saying something he's really not saying! This does not make Bible study a purely academic exercise, but it does mean that true Bible study takes hard and careful work. We'll need to consider things such as context, key words, repeated phrases, structure, and parts of speech. We'll talk a lot more about this later. For now, we'll just say this: to hear God speak, we need to make sure we're getting it right. As we said before, the Bible can never mean something that it never meant.

The Attitude of Bible Study: Humility

We approach written material with a lot of different attitudes. In the grocery store, as you glance at the latest celebrity scandal plastered on the cover of a magazine, you may have an attitude of disgust (hopefully not fascination). When you scan your history textbook as you review for a test, you have a kind of "utilitarian" attitude; you are focusing in on the key points you need to review, and using the textbook to help you master those specific topics. When you read a novel—just for fun, not for an assignment—you probably have the attitude that is closest to the one we should have when studying the Bible; you take in the story and enjoy it. And yet, in Bible study, the primary attitude we ought to have is one of *humility*. If the Bible really is God speaking to us, then our internal monologue as we approach his Word should be, "Lord, I'm listening. Teach me, and help me to obey." We read it to understand it, know it, and enjoy it. Of course, we can be guided in this study by the many great pastors and theologians who have gone before us (and we should!), but every Christian can also look at the Bible for himself or herself and learn what it teaches. But we do so as we place ourselves *under* its authority. We don't stand over it; we allow the Bible to rule and guide our lives and hearts.

A lot of people don't approach the Bible with that attitude. Some people are disgusted by certain parts of the Bible; they don't think that God should punish sin or send people to hell. Some people use the Bible the way you use your history textbook: they take verses out of context to win an argument or back up a political position. Other people genuinely enjoy reading the Bible, but they aren't submitting to its words; they just read it as they'd read a novel. God's people are called to study his Word with an attitude of humility. We sit under it; we don't stand over it.

This attitude toward Bible study is summarized best by Isaiah the prophet. Listen to God's words, as recorded by Isaiah: "This is the one to whom I will look: he who is humble and contrite in spirit and trembles at my word" (Isa. 66:2). When was the last time you had this picture in your head when you thought about a teenage Bible study—a few kids, huddled together in a living room, *trembling* together at God's Word as they humbly listen to it and apply it to their lives? It probably isn't the first picture that popped into your head when you started reading this book. And yet, that's really what Bible study is all about.

This brings us to the very important concept that I'll call "constraint" in Bible study. As we study the Bible, we need to put a certain measure of care—even fear—into letting the text of Scripture lead the way. We must say neither more, nor less, than the text says. As we teach, discuss, and study the Bible, we must guard against anything close to the *abuse* of it, or the use of it for our own agenda or purposes. We must not stand over it; we must be ruled and led and guided by it. The Bible is God speaking; our job is to listen, and to be led by the God who graciously talks to us through his written Word.

DISCUSSION QUESTIONS

WHAT DID WE JUST READ?

1. What do we mean when we say the Bible is "inspired"?

2. What is the difference between "inspiration" and "dictation"?

3. What is the difference between a Bible study that is *personal* and one that is only *propositional*?

SO WHAT?

1. How can you remind yourself that the Bible is not just *about* God, but is actually God speaking to you?

2. How should the fact that the Bible is God speaking make a difference in the way you study it with others?

3. How have you failed to bring the right attitude to Bible study? How can you change your attitude?

2

THE BIBLE IS POWERFUL

"The Bible is useful for both doctrine and life, for creed as well as conduct. It is so useful that it provides total preparation for doing God's will. A Christian who knows the Bible is fully trained to serve God at home, at work, in the church, and everywhere else in a post-Christian culture. In the words of a hymn by James Montgomery Boice, 'God's Word is all the Christian needs to grow in grace and do good deeds.'"

—PHIL RYKEN[1]

HAVE YOU BEEN THERE?

Kiersten had just gotten home from church, and was getting changed before lunch. She couldn't stop thinking about what had just happened. Normally, she tuned out Sunday morning sermons. Not intentionally, of course—but they were often so hard to follow. But this morning had been different.

It wasn't really what the preacher had said, though she actually remembered the main points of his sermon this week. It was the way the words of the Bible passage he preached from had "hit" her. Like a punch in the stomach. She'd read the Bible a lot, of course; she had grown up going to church with her Christian parents. But the words of Scripture had never grabbed her like they had this morning. She couldn't shake the feeling that God himself had spoken those very words to her, as she sat there in her pew. Kiersten kept wondering what this could mean. How could the Bible really hit her with such power? How could words written thousands of years ago affect her in such a significant way? What could that mean about God's written Word?

WORDS OF POWER

We have a dog in our house. She is a big, strong, beautiful English boxer. Her name is Scout. Seventy-five pounds of pure muscle, she can jump several feet in the air and sprint much faster than I can. She's really an amazing creature. But Scout is a bad dog. Sweet, yes. But bad. She gets excited when new people come to our house, and jumps all over them, pawing their clothes. Sometimes, she wants to play so badly that (in good fun, of course) she starts trying to bite my ankles or shoelaces. Scout knows how to sit, but when she gets really wound up, she doesn't listen to anything I say. I have frequently had the experience of almost *yelling* commands at Scout, only to have her completely ignore them and go on acting like a hyper, crazy dog. In my house—to my dog, at least—my words often have very little power!

Contrast this lack of power in my words with the Bible's record of the way God's words functioned in the creation of the world. "In the beginning," we read, "the earth was without form and void, and darkness was over the face of the deep. And the Spirit of God was hovering over the face of the waters" (Gen. 1:1–2). Then something happens in verse 3: "And God *said.*" Have you ever stopped and really considered this? When God created the world, he didn't even get his hands dirty. He *spoke.* He spoke *words.* Powerful words. Words that made things appear out of nothing. This is the God we worship, know, love, and follow. The words of the God of the universe are incredibly powerful; he *spoke* an entire universe into existence. The writer of Hebrews summarizes it this way: "By faith we understand that the universe was created by the word of God, so that what is seen was not made out of things that are visible" (Heb. 11:3).

In short, the words of God are not like human words. Human words, while they can reveal truth, do not have real power behind them. God's words do have power. Real power. Creative power. The God we follow speaks words that get things done.

"The obvious benefit to youth Bible study is that the Word is the means through which the Spirit works. By putting the Bible in front of students time and again it creates opportunity for the Spirit to grip them. I have seen teens grow to be young men and women eager to follow Jesus. Often, though, the benefit is the fruit that is demonstrated years later. Sometimes you'll walk with a teen through four years of small group Bible study, only for them to wander off to college caring nothing for Jesus. But then you run into them five or ten years later and they are grown and passionate and faithful. It is the Word that does that."

—Barnabas Piper (former youth leader, College Church in Wheaton, Illinois)

THE BIBLE: THE POWERFUL WORD OF GOD

In the last chapter, we had an extended discussion about the doctrine of inspiration—the truth that the Bible is actually "breathed out" by God. God used human authors to compose the Bible over almost sixteen centuries, but he inspired them to say exactly what he wanted them to say. Because of this, we can truly say that the Bible is *God speaking.*

If the Bible, then, is God speaking, and God's words (as discussed above) are powerful, then we need to admit that the Bible itself is powerful. Now, when we say that the Bible is powerful, we aren't merely saying that it is extremely profound, moving, or influential, although it certainly is those things. At some time in your life you've probably turned to your friend after seeing a movie in the theater and said, "Wow, that movie was *powerful.*" You meant, maybe, that the movie moved you; it changed your perspective on a particular issue, or emotionally affected you in a powerful way. While the Bible can definitely affect us like that, we are not talking about a mere emotional effect when we discuss the power of the Bible. We are talking about *real* power. Divine power. Listen again to the way the author of Hebrews describes the Word of God: "For the word of God is living and active, sharper than any two-edged sword, piercing to the division of soul and of spirit, of joints and marrow, and discerning the thoughts and intentions of the heart" (Heb. 4:12).

Why is the Bible powerful? Because it is the "living" and "active" Word of God. The Bible is God speaking; it is the very communication of the God who created the universe. It can therefore accomplish things in people's hearts and lives. It can convict. It can open hard hearts. It can actually change people's lives—not metaphorically, but eternally and truly. That is real power.

This power comes to us today in the Bible because the Bible is *still* living. In other words, God the Holy Spirit—who first inspired the words of the Bible—is still very active in speaking to us today through the words that he inspired. The words of Scripture were not inspir*ed* (past tense), they *are* inspired—present tense! Yes, God did breathe Scripture out in the past, but since Scripture is God's Word, it will always be God's Word. This means that God still speaks today through the Bible, which was once "breathed out" by him. The power of Scripture comes from the fact that God's words do not die. God speaks today through his written Word; it is alive. That is why it can accomplish such amazing things in the lives and hearts of human beings.

This is an important point to discuss for a few minutes. The Bible can get things done. God's Word—God's powerful Word—can actually and truly change people's hearts and lives. Now, in a certain sense, this is true of other kinds of literature. I've heard recently about some people who, after reading a couple of different books about adoption, have felt God calling them to adopt children from Africa. The books they read—in a way—changed their lives. What they read had a powerful effect on the way they thought and lived. The movie *Braveheart* (one of my all-time favorites) is powerful; it moves me when I watch it, and it and other movies like it have probably inspired people to be more courageous for certain causes. But no human book, movie, poem, or song has the power of God behind it. Such human creations can have a powerful *effect* on people, but they do not have divine power *in themselves*. The Bible does, because it contains the inspired words of the God whose every word is powerful, life-giving, and effective. Nothing else is inspired in the way the Bible is! Listen again to the amazing things the apostle Paul says the Bible can do:

But as for you, continue in what you have learned and have firmly believed, knowing from whom you learned it and how from childhood you have been acquainted with the sacred writings, which are able to make you wise for salvation through faith in Christ Jesus. All Scripture is breathed out by God and profitable for teaching, for reproof, for correction, and for training in righteousness, that the man of God may be competent, equipped for every good work. (2 Tim. 3:14–17)

Amazingly, the books we carry around to church and to Bible study groups have words in them that are able to make us "wise for salvation." Let me break down the significance of this phrase. It means that reading the Bible can lead you to eternal salvation in Jesus Christ. The words of Scripture can move you to a place of faith in Jesus in which your eternal status before God changes; you go from being under God's wrath and deserving hell to being a child of God, heading to heaven. That is what the Bible can do; it can make you "wise for salvation" through faith in Jesus Christ. There is real power in the words of the Bible, because there is real power when God speaks.

A WORD ON TEACHING

Before we discuss some implications of this truth for Bible study, I want to say a few words to you regarding the teaching that you hear in youth group settings. If the Bible is powerful, then youth leaders should be teaching the Bible. I know that sounds obvious, but I think this is a real problem in youth ministry today. Here's where I think it comes from. Youth leaders, in an attempt to be "relevant," have begun to abandon a true reliance on God's Word and a deep belief in the inherent power of the Bible. They have lost faith in God's ability to get his work done through his inspired, written Word. So they try in all sorts of ways to "spice up" the message. They analyze the newest Lady Gaga song. They show lots of YouTube clips to demonstrate their main points. They poll the group to figure out what topics the youth want to hear talks about. They end up doing lots of series on dating, sex, dancing, and modesty. Talks become more funny, more cute, and seemingly more "relevant" . . . and the Bible plays a less and less prominent role.

Here is what many of us youth leaders have forgotten: the Word of God *alone* holds inherent, divine power to accomplish the saving work of God in people's hearts and lives. God's Word is God's chosen way to get his work done in students' lives. So when we make our talks cute, relevant, and funny—and shove the Bible from its rightfully prominent place in our teaching—we have stopped grounding our teaching in the only truly powerful foundation: God's inspired Word.

Sometimes in our youth group, when we're about to read the passage of Scripture that I'll teach on, I stop and remind the students of an important truth. I tell them that, in the reading of Scripture, they are hearing in the most direct and unmediated way the voice of God. Sure, I'll do my best to explain it clearly and apply it to their lives (that's what preaching means), but as they hear the words of the Bible read, they are hearing God's voice in the clearest way. While preaching is effective, powerful, and necessary in the life of the church, it is only so long as it is faithfully making clear and rightly applying God's powerful Word.

If you're a student, you should absolutely insist on hearing God's Word preached to you. You should not settle for anything less than a youth leader or pastor who gives you the unmediated, powerful, "straight-up" Word of God from the Bible. Don't settle for cute! Don't settle for funny! Don't settle for talks that are seemingly "relevant." Demand to hear God's Word. You deserve to get the good stuff, because Scripture is the only thing that is powerful enough to convict your heart, uncover your sin, and make you wise for salvation in Jesus Christ.

And here's the ironic twist: it's actually God's Word—unmediated—that is the most "relevant" thing of all. In our quest to make our talks relevant, we have lost hold of that truth. If God is our Creator, and we are sinful people in need of a saving relationship with him, then what will be the most eternally relevant thing to us? Hearing God speak. That's the most relevant thing—to hear God's voice, speaking to us today, telling us the words of salvation, grace, and truth. Youth leaders, build your ministries and your teaching on the Word of God. It is powerful, living, active, and eternally relevant. Students, demand nothing less than the living and active Word of God. Nothing else has the power to grip your heart and lead you further in faith in Jesus Christ.

IMPLICATIONS FOR BIBLE STUDY

The Bible is powerful. That's what we've been talking about. The inspired Word of God has within itself inherent power: God speaks, and God always speaks powerfully. If this is true, then we need to think about some important implications for our *attitudes* concerning God's Word—especially in relation to Bible study.

A Respect for the Words

If the written and inspired Word of God—the Bible—is powerful, then we should respect it. We should hold it in reverence, listen to it carefully, and place it above our own egos, agendas, and personal interests. One of the pastors on our staff at College Church has been serving our congregation for a long time. He is an extremely godly man—someone that all of us younger pastors really look up to (I won't name him because I don't want to embarrass him; he's very humble). One of the other younger guys on staff summarized our attitude toward this pastor very well the other day. He said, "When he speaks, we all listen." In other words, there is a deep respect that we have for this man. In a staff meeting, when he addresses an issue, we all get very quiet, because we know that he'll approach the issue with wisdom, careful thought, and insight gained from years of ministry experience. In a much greater way, we ought to honor and respect the powerful Word of God. When God speaks through his Word, we should shut up and listen. We should have the deepest respect for the Bible.

But I also used the plural—"words"—intentionally in the heading of this section. We need to have a deep respect for the Word of God, but also for the *words* that God the Holy Spirit has intentionally chosen to make up his written Word. Let's remember together that the Bible, as originally written down, was mainly in Hebrew (the Old Testament) and Greek (the New Testament). The Scriptures were not written down in outline form, the way that you might get a handout for a lecture that gives you an idea about where the teacher is going with the lesson. The Scriptures were inspired by God wholly. They were then recorded, under God's sovereign direction, in word-by-word fashion by the human authors. God takes words seriously! Listen to what John, in the book of Revelation, says about the seriousness of the specific words that make up his record of the vision God gave him:

> I warn everyone who hears the words of the prophecy of this book: if anyone adds to them, God will add to him the plagues described in this book, and if anyone takes away from the words of the book of this prophecy, God will take away his share in the tree of life and in the holy city, which are described in this book. (Rev. 22:18–19)

God gave his special revelation to us, through divinely inspired human authors, through the medium of carefully and specifically chosen words. I'll say it again: God takes his words very seriously. So should we. So, let's think about a couple of ways that we can respect the words that God has given to us in the Bible.

First, we should be very careful to stick closely to the words of the Bible. Far too often—especially in the context of Bible study—we move way too quickly into a neat and tidy "summary" of what we *think* a Bible verse or passage is saying. In doing that, there is often a danger of glossing over difficult words and making them mean what we think they should mean. We can, when we do this, miss the importance of a word that makes us uncomfortable, but is there in the text for a specific purpose.

Consider, for example, the very well-known passage Romans 3:23–25, which is one of the clearest summaries of the message of the gospel. You are probably familiar with this passage:

> For all have sinned and fall short of the glory of God, and are justified by his grace as a gift, through the redemption that is in Christ Jesus, whom God put forward as a propitiation by his blood, to be received by faith.

Now, the "big picture" of these verses is evident, right? We're sinners, so we fall short of God's glory. We're saved by God's grace alone—through Jesus, who died on the cross for us. But what have we missed when we summarized these verses in that (true) way? We've missed a very difficult and uncomfortable word in the passage: the word "propitiation." Now, it's easier not to deal with that word, right? We get the big idea of what the passage is saying, so why get caught up on a long, confusing, "theological" term? Well, the answer to that question is (and must always be), "Because God put that word there on purpose!" Respecting God's Word, and all the

40

"words" in God's Word, means that we wrestle with all of them, knowing that God has put them there intentionally for our benefit and our understanding of him. In this case, the word "propitiation" has a very specific meaning; it has to do with the removal of wrath. The picture that it presents is one of Jesus soaking up—drinking, even—all the wrath that God has toward sin, to the extent that God actually doesn't have any wrath left for us. That is an amazing, striking, violent picture of Jesus' death on the cross, isn't it? He forgives us, yes, but he forgives us by "drinking" all the wrath of God so that all that violent wrath is actually removed from us, the people who deserve it most! In this case, the specific, difficult word that we may have wanted to avoid is the key to the fuller picture of the grace of Jesus on the cross that this passage is meant to give us. Respect the words! Wrestle with them! It will be worth it.

Second, we can't avoid some brief comments on Bible translations here. We need to realize that all our Bibles (assuming we're reading them in English) are not in their original languages. They have been translated into English from Hebrew and Greek. And when a book is translated, some things will always be "lost in translation." Some of the humor, rhymes, or subtle ironies of the original language won't come through in a different language. Translators of Scripture must make decisions about how to translate difficult phrases or ideas into English—or any other language. So, how should a respect for the words of the Bible make a difference in what Bible translation we read, study, or teach from?

I want to urge you, when you're considering which English translation to use for Bible study, to choose a translation whose translating team has used an "essentially literal" approach to translation, rather than an approach that is called "dynamic equivalence." Whoa—hold on! What does that mean??? I'll tell you. An essentially literal translation (like the English

Standard Version or the New American Standard Version) tries to translate the Hebrew and Greek words as literally as possible into English—even if that means that some words or phrases sound a bit outdated or awkward. This is because the people working on these translations are trying to do everything they can to hold on to the actual words that the biblical authors used. They also try to do this consistently. So, for example, if the Greek word *kurios* is translated "Lord" in one chapter of a book in the Bible, they'll try to translate that word the same way in the rest of the book. This helps us—reading the book in English—see that the Greek writer was using the same Greek word. That can be *very* beneficial in a small group study!

Practitioners of the translation approach called "dynamic equivalence" seek to translate the main idea of a phrase, rather than the specific words that make up the phrase. The most notable translation in this category is the New International Version, and more recently, Today's New International Version. This approach is almost always helpful, and many brilliant Christian leaders and scholars have used it when translating the Bible. They argue for it on the basis of linguistics, mainly. Imagine, for example, that you're trying to explain to a French person how to ask for directions to the bathroom in English. In French, one would ask, "Ou est la salle de bain?" Literally translated into English, that would be, "Where is the room of bath?" Now, you would probably argue that to teach your friend to say, "Where's the bathroom?" would not only be more normal-sounding, it would actually be a *better translation*. And you would be right. Many times, brilliant translators do a great job getting the right idea of a biblical passage across using the dynamic equivalence approach. But there are two main problems with this approach to Bible translation.

First, and perhaps most obviously, sometimes even brilliant people get it wrong! Some scholars, in their attempt to get across not the literal words of the Greek text but the meaning of the text, mess it up—and end up translating something that the actual words weren't saying. Consider a striking example from John 11:6. Jesus has just heard that his dear friend Lazarus— brother of Mary and Martha—is extremely ill. John 11:5 tells us that Jesus loved Martha and Mary and Lazarus. Now, listen to what comes in 11:6—and note the significant difference between the NIV and ESV translations of the verse's first word:

> NIV—"Yet when he heard that Lazarus was sick, he stayed where he was two more days."

> ESV—"So, when he heard that Lazarus was ill, he stayed two days longer in the place where he was."

Do you see the important difference? That's right—the NIV starts with the word "yet," and the ESV starts with the word "so." What's the big deal? Well, you remember that, just one verse before, John has told us how much Jesus loves Lazarus and his sisters. We have to make sense, then, of the fact that Jesus doesn't come rushing to them when he hears Lazarus is sick. The NIV, trying to get across the big idea of the verse, uses the word "yet"—in other words, Jesus stays where he is a bit longer, *in spite* of his great love for these women and this man. The ESV, on the other hand, goes with the literal translation of the Greek word *oun*, which is almost always translated "therefore," or "so." It looks like, according to the actual word that is used in the Greek, it is precisely Jesus' love for Lazarus and his sisters that *motivates* him to stay two days longer where he is. In other words, Jesus loves them so much that he intentionally lets Lazarus die, so that he can show them his resurrection power by raising Lazarus from the dead. He does this *because* he loves them, not *in spite* of the fact that he loves them. He loves them so much, in fact, that he wants to show them his glory, even if it means allowing them to go through an incredibly painful experience.

Rather than relying on the translation of the actual word that is used in this verse, the translators of the NIV tried to make sense of this on their own, and they ended up, to some extent, missing the point of what Jesus was doing in this passage.

The second problem of the dynamic equivalence approach is a bit more subtle, and it applies even when the translators "get it right." Here's the problem: getting it right (in other words, correctly interpreting the main idea of a passage or verse in the Bible) is *our* job as students and teachers of the Bible! It is *not* the job of the translator. A Bible translation should give us the *words*—the actual words that were written, sticking as closely as possible to their literal meanings. We need to then commit ourselves to a careful, dutiful, sometimes tedious study of the Bible, in order to figure out the big idea and main application of any part of it. Dynamic equivalence–based translations take that work—that wonderful work—out of our hands. They do it with good intentions! But they do some of the work of careful Bible study and interpretation as a part of their translation.

Now, I know I've been speaking rather forcefully about this issue. A lot of you use the NIV, and many wonderful people, churches, and seminaries use it as well. I grew up reading, studying, and hearing preaching from the NIV. Some of you like reading the New Living Translation (NLT), and some of you may even think it's helpful to read the "Message." I'm not saying you should never look at those other translations. In fact, it can be very valuable to see the interpretive work that various experts and Bible scholars have done on various passages of Scripture. What I am saying is that you shouldn't assume that you're getting the most literal translation of the words from the original languages, if you read and study a translation that is not "essentially literal." You will be reading someone else's interpretation of the text, not the closely literal translation of the text itself. In the case of the NLT and the "Message," you'll actually be reading someone's paraphrase of the text. Again, I'm not saying it's bad to read these, but for intense Bible study, I'd highly recommend reading an English version that employs the essentially literal translation approach.

The Sufficiency of the Words

A second implication of this idea we've been discussing— that the Bible is powerful—is the sufficiency of the words of Scripture. Now, this doctrine of the sufficiency of Scripture has been often misused and frequently misunderstood. Some critics of this doctrine have assumed that those who believe that Scripture is sufficient believe that the Bible teaches us everything we can know about everything in the world. They take it to be a slap in the face of scientific experimentation and technological development, historical research, and medical advances. Let me be clear: saying that the words of the Bible are sufficient is not saying that the Bible teaches us every-thing there is to know about anything. The Bible does not, for example, teach us Newton's laws, or the Pythagorean Theorem, or even the fact that seven times five equals thirty-five. There is much learning that we can do about God's creation that takes place outside the pages of Scripture.

To say that the words of the Bible are sufficient is to say that the Bible is *enough*. The words of Scripture are enough to bring us knowledge of God, an understanding of our sinfulness, and full comprehension of the life-giving gospel of Jesus Christ, with all its implications for every part of our lives. The Bible is—eternally—enough. And it is sufficient to give us full knowledge, then, of what is most eternally valuable: who God is, and how we can be in an eternal relationship with him. It is enough to give us saving knowledge of God; it is all we need to know how to relate rightly to our Creator.

In Bible study, then, we need to embrace and understand the sufficiency of Scripture. We can say goodbye to the need we feel sometimes to "supplement" the Bible with stories, experiences, or related news clips. Of course, illustrations are not always bad, but we need to realize and remind ourselves that the Bible—God's *powerful* Word—is enough to engage people, convict them, and speak to their hearts in a powerful, even saving, way.

Teenage students, hear me on this point: the Bible is *enough*. God's Word is enough to bring you to a saving knowledge of Jesus, and it is enough to give you wisdom, strength, and guidance to live for Jesus every day of your life. If you don't know that, believe that, and feel that in your heart, then you may not have yet understood the gospel and really "heard" God's Word speak to you. If you do know, believe, and feel that God's Word is enough for you, start acting like it! Stop trying to "spice up" the Bible; just let it speak. Let it speak to you, first, in your own personal study. Then unleash it and let God speak to the people around you in your Bible studies, accountability huddles, and youth groups. Get ready, too, because powerful things may happen when we get out of God's way, and let the Bible start doing the talking!

DISCUSSION QUESTIONS

WHAT DID WE JUST READ?

1. How did God create the world? What does that tell us about his words?

2. What does it mean that God's word is *powerful?* What kind of power is in his words?

3. What are the two different approaches to Bible translation discussed in this chapter? How might your choice of Bible translation affect your Bible study?

4. What does it mean to say the Bible is *sufficient?*

SO WHAT?

1. What would it look like in your life if you really believed that God's Word is the most powerful thing around?

2. What are some ways we "get in the way" of God's Word in Bible studies or in youth group?

3. What are some ways that you could respect God's Word (and words) even more?

4. Do you really believe that the Bible is enough to help you know God and follow him? Why is it hard to believe that?

3

THE BIBLE IS UNDERSTANDABLE

"All things in Scripture are not alike plain in themselves, nor alike clear unto all: yet those things which are necessary to be known, believed, and observed for salvation are so clearly propounded, and opened in some place of Scripture or other, that not only the learned, but the unlearned, in a due use of the ordinary means, may attain unto a sufficient understanding of them."
—WESTMINSTER CONFESSION OF FAITH 1.7

HAVE YOU BEEN THERE?

Luke loved going to church. Because of this, he sometimes felt that he was very different from his peers, who sat through church services with bored expressions on their faces and eyes glazed over with disinterest. Luke, though, loved listening to his pastor. The man was a great

49

preacher—engaging, humorous, and deep, too. He had not only attended seminary, but had gone overseas for a few years to earn his doctorate in theology from a prominent school in England. Luke admired him, and loved the insights into Scripture that he gained from his preaching. Week after week, he walked away from church thinking to himself, "Wow! I'm glad I heard that, because I *never* could have figured out what that passage was talking about!" He was just glad he had a pastor who could make the Bible make sense to him, because Luke knew he could never understand it that clearly on his own. The Bible, really, was like a mystery to him. Luke figured that was just the way it was—and that's why we all need pastors!

WORDS OF MYSTERY?

For hundreds of years, even well into the sixteenth century, church leaders insisted that the Bible should be read in church in *Latin*. This meant that priests and bishops had to be trained in Latin in order to lead—and it also meant the most ordinary people sitting in the pews of the church had almost no idea what was going on in the church service! Most people weren't well educated, and certainly didn't know Latin. It took a major Reformation, spearheaded by men like Martin Luther, to initiate the translation of the Bible first into German, and then into many other languages. Luther's translation of the entire Bible into German was finally completed in 1534; it was his crowning lifework. For him, it was the result of an intense desire to get God's Word into the hands of the ordinary people in the pews of the church. All people, he believed, should have access to the Bible in a language that they understood. The Bible should be accessible and available to every single Christian!

You see, for those in the church who insisted on only using the Latin Scriptures in church worship, there was more going on than just a preference for that language. It was a power play; it helped them stay in control of the people by keeping them in the dark about what the Bible really said. With the Bible—and the knowledge it contains about God and his people—kept a mystery to the general public, church leaders had relative freedom to lead how they liked and to do what they wanted. It was precisely this attitude and intention that Luther protested, and we still reap the benefits of his Reformation in our churches today.

Here's the good news for us today: God's Word is *not meant to be a mystery to us.* In fact, one of the great gifts God gives us in his Word is that it is clear and understandable. God is not like those church leaders who gained control by keeping people in the dark about Scripture. God wants us to know him and to understand his Word! We have a Bible in our hands today that is not mysterious, tricky, or written in some undecipherable divine code. It is clear, straightforward, and understandable. God means for his people to "get" his Word.

Listen to these wise words by Wayne Grudem, a professor at Phoenix Seminary:

> Sometimes seminary students have a false impression that when they come to seminary they will be given some 'secret tools' for getting hidden meaning from the text that other people couldn't find there. But this is not true, because the Bible was written for ordinary people, and it was written in the ordinary language of the people to whom it was first given. That is why Moses could command all the people of Israel, "These words that I command you today shall be on your heart. You shall teach them diligently to your children, and shall talk of them when you sit in your house,

and when you walk by the way, and when you lie down, and when you rise."[1]

In other words, the Bible—God's Word—was always intended to be understandable. That was God's purpose for the ancient Israelites when they received his Law. That is his intention for us today, as we receive, learn, and study his written Word. The Bible is a book for real life; we are supposed to understand it clearly.

Theologians call this idea we're discussing the *perspicuity* of Scripture. They mean that the necessary truths and doctrines of the Bible—about God, Jesus, sin, and salvation—can be correctly and clearly understood by any human being of ordinary intelligence. Does this mean that there aren't difficult parts of the Bible that are hard to understand? Of course not! There are parts of the Bible that theologians and scholars still wrestle over—and will continue to debate until Jesus returns. But the central truths of the Bible, the doctrine of perspicuity teaches, can be easily and clearly understood.

This doesn't mean, of course, that any Christian who reads the Bible will automatically become an expert on it. If that were true, then pastors shouldn't go to seminary, and we wouldn't have any need for Sunday school, discipleship, Bible classes, or even Christian books about the Bible! Study is important, because there is certainly always more that we can learn about the Bible. Here's how John Frame sums up this idea of the "clarity" of Scripture in his book on God's Word:

> I conclude this as an important principle: *Scripture is always clear enough for us to carry out our present responsibilities before God.* It is clear enough for a six-year-old to understand what God expects of him. It is also clear enough for a mature theologian to understand what God expects of him. . . .

Scripture is not exhaustively clear to anyone. It is not clear enough to satisfy anyone who merely wants to gain a speculative knowledge of divine things. It is, rather, morally sufficient, practically sufficient, sufficient for each person to know what God desires of him.[2]

Do you see what he's saying? He's telling us that the Bible is always clear enough to guide us and speak to us *wherever we are* in our walk with Jesus Christ. The Bible is clear! It's deep enough for professional theologians to spend lifetimes wrestling with its truths and mysteries, and yet accessible enough for a young child to grasp its basic teachings and concepts. We can always go deeper in our study and understanding of Scripture. But that does not mean that what God wants us to know about him is not immediately clear to us from a simple reading of his Word. It is.

IMPLICATIONS FOR BIBLE STUDY

The Main Point

The implications of all this theology we've been doing are hugely important for the actual practice of Bible study. If we really believe in the *perspicuity* of Scripture—that the Bible is overwhelmingly "understandable" to the average human being—then all of a sudden we can be filled with a lot of confidence as we begin to study it. We can *get* the Bible! God intends us to get it. The Bible is not a code that we need an ordained minister to somehow "crack" for us; the Bible is right there, accessible to us. Teenagers: the Bible is accessible to *you*. Remember Professor Grudem's words above: Scripture isn't just for seminary students with some secret knowledge or insight. Bible study and interpretation is for everyone who gives himself or herself to it.

If this is true, your first task when you study the Bible is to work hard to find the main point of the passage you're studying. There is always a main point! Yes, there are subpoints, tangents, applications, and illustrations. But remember, the Bible is a divine book, but also a *human* book. Human authors wrote Scripture as they were inspired by the Holy Spirit, and they wrote to make a *point!* Listen to Professor Grudem on this subject:

> What we are looking for as we read Scripture is *understanding*. We seek to know what the words and the phrases *mean*. . . . In all this we are asking God to give us *understanding*. We want to know *why* a sentence means one thing and not another; and we believe that the reasons for a certain meaning will be there in the text if we look for them until we find them.[3]

When you look at a passage of the Bible—in a group or on your own—and study it carefully, your goal should always be to find the main point that the author was trying to communicate to the original audience. That is usually not too complicated; we often make it a lot more mysterious than it needs to be! There are some good and practical ways that we can get to the main point of a passage. But before we go there, we need to make one important clarification.

Hard Work

My wife has run five marathons. That's right—five! She's also had two children, and she works a part-time job from home. She is an amazing woman! I think one thing she has told me about running marathons applies directly to Bible study. "Anybody can run a marathon," she told me once. Now, there are obviously some people who are simply not physically healthy enough, so this was a bit of an exaggeration. But she went on to explain that any relatively healthy person, who will commit to a disciplined plan of marathon training, can slowly work up the endurance and strength necessary to complete a 26.2-mile race. Anyone can do it! But it takes a great amount of commitment and consistency.

"Getting" the Bible can be a bit like running a marathon. When we say that the Bible is understandable and that anyone can study it and "get" it, we don't necessarily mean that Bible study will always be *easy*. In fact, while God means for us to *get* the Bible, it often takes some diligent study and commitment to understand what the Bible is teaching us. Friends, Bible study can sometimes be *very hard work*! It's hard work that can be done by anybody willing to make the commitment, but it will sometimes take some mental "sweat" to understand and apply the riches that are contained in the Bible. God's Word is worth the effort; I hope you're willing to discipline yourself to get into it!

If you're not a runner, here's another way to look at it. Reading and understanding the Bible is a little bit like riding a bike. Many children learn how to ride a bike while they are still very small, and unable to go very fast. Similarly, anyone can begin reading and studying the Bible! It takes a lot of time, commitment, and discipline, though, to become a cyclist in the Tour de France. The basic skills, learned at a very young age, are developed, honed, and practically perfected. Friends, are you ready to devote that kind of discipline, practice, and effort to reading and understanding God's Word? I hope you are!

FINDING THE MAIN POINT OF A PASSAGE

Now we come to the nitty-gritty part of this chapter—the practical tips for studying the Bible. I've tried to show you that the Bible is understandable. I've urged you that the first goal, given the Bible's perspicuity, is to try to find the main point of any passage you're studying. So . . . how in the world do we start trying to find the main point?

Repeated Words or Phrases

Imagine that you're out on a school night with your friends, and you end up staying out much later than you should have. You crawl into bed after midnight, and when your alarm clock (or cell phone) goes off at six o'clock the next morning, you barely even hear it. Your mother, busy with work around the house, finds you still asleep in bed at 7:35 a.m. . . . five minutes after school has already begun! She proceeds to give you this speech:

> I can't believe you slept through your alarm again. That is so completely irresponsible. Your father and I are trying to teach you responsibility, but at some point, you're going to need to begin making decisions for yourself. What are you going to do in college, when you have to be responsible for getting yourself to class every day?

Now, aside from the obvious tone of disappointment and frustration in that "speech," what is a big hint about the main point that is in your mother's mind? It's the repetition of some form of the word "responsibility," isn't it? In fact, in just four short sentences, she used that word three times. It's the notion of responsibility that is driving your mother's speech to you; she wants you to have it, and in her opinion, you don't!

Often in the Bible, the writers are almost as obvious as your mother in their repetition of a main idea, word, or phrase. They have a main point, and they'll repeat certain things again and again that direct you to that main idea. Consider the following passage:

Not that I have already obtained this or am already perfect, but I press on to make it my own, because Christ Jesus has made me his own. Brothers, I do not consider that I have made it my own. But one thing I do: forgetting what lies behind and straining forward to what lies ahead, I press on toward the goal for the prize of the upward call of God in Christ Jesus. (Phil. 3:12–14)

These are three very rich verses from the writing of Paul! So, how would we begin homing in on the main point? Well, there is one main idea that Paul seems to keep repeating: the idea of *pressing on* or *straining forward*. "I press on," he says in verse 12. "Straining forward," he says in verse 13. "I press on," he says again in verse 14. Paul is focused on a forward-facing, pushing-ahead kind of idea in these verses. So, just by looking at some repeated ideas, we've already begun to find our way to Paul's main point in this passage: Christians need to avoid complacency in their faith, and keep "pressing on" to know Christ better and to one day see him face to face.

Top and Tail

I wrote a note to a couple from our church the other day that went something like this:

Dear Mr. and Mrs. So-and-So,
    I want to thank you so much for having me to lunch the other day. It was wonderful to be in your home, and to get to know you both better. I'm so excited that you're going to be a part of our ministry this year at the church, and I look forward to serving Christ together. Again, thank you so much for a wonderful meal in your home.
    Blessings,
    Jon

That's not a long note, but I said a few different things, didn't I? I talked about the couple's home. I mentioned the ministry where we serve together in the church. What is a big hint, though, about the main point of that letter? It's the way I both began and ended it—with a word of *thanks* for the meal. I know this is a pretty obvious example; the letter was a thank-you note. But you get the point. Another good way to get to the heart of a biblical writer's main point in a passage or book is to look at how he both begins and ends. I sometimes refer to this tool as the "top and tail" method. What "tops" or begins the passage? What is the "tail," or the end, of the passage? Let's consider an example of this, this time from the Old Testament.

In 1 Samuel 22, the first five verses of the chapter describe David—not yet king, and still on the run from Saul, who is trying to kill him. Hiding in a cave, David begins to attract all kinds of outcasts, misfits, debtors, and outlaws. They come to him and find *safety* with him. The bulk of the chapter—verses 6 to 19—goes on to describe the volatile King Saul mercilessly slaughtering eighty-five of God's priests, because one of them had helped David escape. Then, in the last few verses of the chapter, the author takes us back to David. One priest gets away from Saul's slaughter, and David takes him in and protects him; this runaway finds *safety* with David. What is the author doing? He is intentionally beginning and ending this passage with a picture of *the safety that God's true king David provides*. This is in stark contrast to the murderous rage of Saul. In this case, the "top and tail" of the passage direct us to the main point: God's true king, David, gives *safety* to God's people who are in danger.

Purpose Statement

Sometimes people don't leave any room for confusion regarding the main point of their communication. I got a call once from our church's director of administration. "Jon," she said, "I need to talk to you about the incident on the youth retreat last week." A student had taken a nasty fall on the tubing hill at our winter retreat, and she needed to make sure that the family had been notified properly, and that no medical attention had been necessary. There was no doubt in my mind what the main point of our conversation would be when I went down to her office; she had provided me with a "purpose statement" for our talk!

Sometimes, biblical writers are that obvious—and helpfully so. In many books in the Bible, writers actually just *tell us* what their purpose is. We shouldn't miss the main point in these cases! The short letter of Jude is a good example of this. Listen to how Jude begins his letter: "Beloved, although I was very eager to write to you about our common salvation, I found it necessary to write appealing to you to contend for the faith that was once for all delivered to the saints" (v. 3).

If you're doing a Bible study on the book of Jude, and you are veering too far away from the theme of "contending for the faith," you know you've missed the mark! Jude tells us the main point of his letter; he wants God's people to contend for the faith. His purpose statement should direct us as we study his letter, and our interpretation and application should line up with it.

Key Words (the "Therefore" Rule)

Sometimes it's the little tiny words—the "ifs, buts, and fors"—that can be the key to finding the main point in a passage of the Bible. Those transitional words can be extremely important. The word "therefore," for example, is often a big hint about the writer's meaning, purpose, and main point. You've heard the old line, I'm sure: "Whenever you see a 'therefore,' stop and ask what it is *there for!*" A bit corny, I know, but it's a good reminder. Here's a good example: "I appeal to you therefore, brothers, by the mercies of God, to present your bodies as a living sacrifice, holy and acceptable to God, which is your spiritual worship" (Rom. 12:1).

When you're studying Romans 12, that "therefore" should stop you in your tracks. Paul is using that word very intentionally. He is telling us that this command—to "present" our bodies to God as living sacrifices—is *grounded* in everything that has come before in his letter. All the rich theology of salvation by grace, through faith, by the "mercies" of God—all of this is the foundation for the command that he is now giving. Romans 12:1, then, is the *result* or *application* of everything that Paul has said in the book of Romans up to this point. In a Bible study, getting the main point of this passage means relating it to everything that has come before. That little word "therefore" clues us in to that.

Conclusion

Friends, the Bible is there to be studied and understood. You can do it! Hopefully, these simple and practical hints or "tools" will get you off to a good start in finding your way to the main point of any passage in the Bible that you want to study. It will often take some hard work; you've got to pay attention to details, purpose statements, tops and tails, and connecting words. But if you put in some sweat, you'll find that you will begin to dig into the great riches that God's Word has for us today.

DISCUSSION QUESTIONS

WHAT DID WE JUST READ?

1. What does it mean to speak about the *perspicuity* of the Bible? Why is this an important doctrine for us to embrace?

2. What are some key ways to begin identifying the main point of a Bible passage?

3. What does the human authorship of the Bible tell us about the existence of a main point?

SO WHAT?

1. How should the *perspicuity* of the Bible encourage us as we study it?

2. How can we put in more "sweat" and effort as we study the Bible?

3. How can we do a better job finding the main point of the Bible passages we study?

4

THE BIBLE IS A LITERARY WORK

"If the Bible is indeed God speaking, then we do well to listen with full and utmost attention to every detail. If it is true that God is the original word-speaker and that every human being uses words only because of the image of God in him, then anything about words, including their literary beauty, has to do with God. We all (not just 'literary people' but all of us) need to pay more attention to words."

—KATHLEEN NIELSON[1]

HAVE YOU BEEN THERE?

Sarah had always loved reading and studying the Bible. In fact, she considered those activities the ones that had been most beneficial to her growth in Christ. Even when she was younger, she had read with fascination the stories of the Old Testament and the writings of the New Testament, eager to gain new insights about the God she served. Sarah had a very high view of Scripture; if the Bible said it, she believed it! She loved discovering more and more of the wonderful truths revealed in the pages of God's Word. Then, one day, a guest speaker in her Sunday school class began to probe into the poetic elements of one of the psalms. She spoke about rhythm, images, metaphors, and figures of speech. It was as if she were *analyzing* the psalm in an academic way. This really bothered Sarah! The speaker eventually got to the meaning of the psalm, and applied it to the Christian life in what seemed to be a right and valid way, but something still seemed wrong. Can we really "analyze" Scripture like that? Sarah thought it seemed disrespectful to Scripture to do so. Shouldn't we just see what the Bible has to teach us about God, rather than digging into the specific literary forms it uses and the details of the writing style? Can we really read the Bible the way we read other kinds of literature?

LITERATURE—WHAT IS IT?

You read a lot of things in any given day, even if you don't consider yourself much of a reader. If you're a sports fan, you may read the scrolling baseball scores from the night before at the bottom of the television screen on ESPN's *SportsCenter*. While you're driving to school, or riding the bus, you will (maybe subconsciously) read billboard advertisements, store signs, and the little electronic boards at banks and schools telling you the time and the outside temperature. At some point in the last few months, you probably received a letter. Maybe it was a birthday card from your grandma, or an informational letter from your school. I think I've made my point: you all read all the time, even when you're not really thinking about it!

But, even though you read all the time, you automatically shift gears and read *in a different way* when you pick up a work of fiction. Many of you probably read *The Hunger Games* when it came out (or something since then that was just as popular); it was quite a craze! When you picked up that book, you read it with different eyes—a different attitude—than you use when casually reading a billboard advertisement, or the headline on a magazine cover in the grocery store. Why? Because a novel is *literature*. It belongs to a completely different category of writing, and so you read it in a different way. You read it for more than information; you read it to be captured by the story. You want to enjoy it—to feel the emotions of the characters and experience the ups and downs of the plot. Reading literature is different than reading a birthday card from your grandma!

Listen to the way that Wheaton College professor Leland Ryken talks about literature:

> There is no more foundational literary principle than that the subject of literature is human experience concretely presented. Literature incarnates its meaning and ideas into concrete form. . . . The chief means by which literature communicates the very quality of experiences is concreteness of expression. In literature we constantly encounter the sights and sounds of real life.[2]

Literature, in other words, is *concrete*. It's real. It's connected to human experience, and it is intended to show us human experience with richness, expression, and creativity. In this way, literature is different from a cookbook, an advertisement, or a sports game's box score.

The Bible As Literature

Friends, the Bible is *literature*. It is a distinctly *literary* work. Let that thought settle on you for a few moments. What are some other ways we tend to think about the Bible? As a list of rules, maybe, like you might find in a student handbook. As a record of information and facts, similar to a textbook—a format that's all too familiar! Maybe you already have a good grasp of the fact that the Bible is God's communication to us, but you don't often think about it as a distinctly literary sort of communication. Yet that's what the Bible is—a literary work.

Think for a moment what this tells us about our God. He could have given his revelation to us in lists, or in tables and graphs, or he could have simply planted it like a chip into our brains. But he used carefully formed words, which come to us in the form of literature. And what words they are! They come to us in story, in poetry, in letters, and in song. We learn his truth through images, metaphors, graphic language, and carefully formed narratives—stories told by gifted storytellers. There is variation here. Different genres and voices emerge from distinct times and places. It is all God's truth—all his communication—and yet it is delivered with artistry and variation. Our God is an artist. Our God is a *writer*.

As you ponder that thought, listen again to Professor Ryken, who is one of the leading scholars studying the Bible as literature:

> The Bible is a largely literary book. It comes to us in the form of distinct genres, each with its own conventions and craft. . . . We can simply look at the works that the biblical writers composed in order to confirm that they were literary craftsmen. Biblical storytellers knew how to shape well-made plots and to paint vivid characters. Biblical poets had mastered the dynamics of metaphor and simile.[3]

He goes on to quote C. S. Lewis, who says, "There is a . . . sense in which the Bible, since it is after all literature, cannot properly be read except as literature; and the different parts of it as the different sorts of literature they are."[4] God, in his perfect, divine artistry and creativity, chose to give us his Word by inspiring human authors who wrote literature. His communication comes to us in an obviously *literary* work.

It's a literary work, too, composed by *human beings who were literarily crafting their writing*. Here's what I mean by this. Moses, the author of at least a good portion of the first five books of the Bible, could have merely written down the facts of God's people's story. It could even have been like a timeline, or a diary of events:

> 8:00 a.m.: Woke up, ate some manna; people seemed grumpy.
> 9:00 a.m.: People started grumbling more.
> 10:00 a.m.: Got frustrated; decided to pray to God.
> 11:30 a.m.: Things getting ugly . . . these people are driving me crazy!

But that's nothing like what we find in the historical books written by Moses. What do we find there? Stories! Carefully crafted narratives. Moses was intentionally telling the story of God's people, not only with attention to factual accuracy, but with *literary care*. And that's precisely how God chooses to give his Word to us—and this does not at all interfere with God's inspiration of the Bible! In fact, this is what makes his sovereign inspiration of Scripture all the more amazing. He makes sure that his Scripture is exactly how he wants it to be, and he has seen fit to allow the human authors, like Moses, to shape their writing in beautifully literary ways.

Or consider the mere existence of the book of Psalms. Yes, we certainly learn truths about God by reading and studying the psalms. We learn history, too, since some psalms recount the actions of God throughout the experience of his people. But at their core, the psalms are poems. Songs. Composed by human beings who were carried along by the

Holy Spirit (i.e., *inspired*), but who were also carefully and creatively crafting songs for God's people. They put words together with purpose—with attention to detail, beauty, rhythm, and allusion. The amazing fact about this, again, is that God chose to inspire the Bible in this way! As Peter puts it in 2 Peter 1:21, "Men spoke from God as they were carried along by the Holy Spirit."

Even Paul's letters are literary in nature. Yes, they tend to be the most densely theological parts of the Bible, but it's obvious that Paul was writing with careful precision, artistry, and literary awareness. He didn't have to do that. Paul could have sent checklists to churches, or long sets of instructions. But he didn't. He sat down and deliberately—literarily—penned thoughtful and carefully worded letters, not only to instruct early believers in the Christian faith, but to appeal to their emotions as well.

I could go on, but I won't! We'll talk much more about the different kinds of literature that we see in the Bible in our chapter on the different biblical genres. For now, you see the point I'm making: the Bible is *literature*.

Avoiding Extremes

This entire conversation is making some of you uncomfortable, and you may even be thinking to yourself, "This guy is a heretic!" If that's the case, then you may have been living in one of the "extremes" that I'm trying to call attention to here. That extreme is this: you read the Bible to teach you about God, because you believe this is the primary purpose of Scripture. And, basically, you're right! But that narrow focus you take when reading and studying the Bible makes you feel uncomfortable with even *admitting* the literary nature of the Bible. To you, talking about the way that the biblical authors chose specific words, or shaped stories, or intentionally "turned a phrase," all sound like ways that people might be led to minimize the inspiration and authority of Scripture. After all, isn't the Bible *God's* Word, not *people's* words? Well, yes. But that doesn't mean that God didn't choose to work *specifically and intentionally through the human personalities, skills, and writing abilities of the Bible's human authors.* In fact, that *is* how God chose to work. And the result of that surprising, condescending act of God is a Bible that is, at its very core, literary. To study the Bible for theological truth is right, of course. But to recognize its literary nature is to understand clearly the mystery of the doctrine of inspiration. God chose to communicate his truth to this world *through distinct human personalities, writing styles, and literary genres.*

Of course we also need to avoid the other extreme. Secular colleges and universities all around the country have adopted this approach, reading the Bible *only* as literature, studying it in *exactly* the same way that we study Shakespeare, Plato, or Homer, or any other old piece of literature. People who do this often come to some right conclusions about what a particular text, psalm, or epistle is saying, but they don't do the very thing that God has designed the Bible to make us do: believe it as God's very Word. To study the Bible *only* as literature is to miss the most important truth about it: that it is the inspired and authoritative Word of the Creator God. Even as we study its literary qualities carefully, we are always supposed to be putting ourselves under its authority and power. It's literary, yes, but it is still *God* speaking.

So . . . what in the world does all this mean for Bible study?

Reading for More Than Propositions

First and foremost, recognizing that the Bible is literature impacts the way we read it. Think back to our earlier example, of a fiction novel. How do you read a novel? Do you read a novel just to get the facts—to memorize characters' names, understand details of the plot, and learn vocabulary words that the author uses to tell the story? Maybe, but only if you're required to read the novel for an English class at school! If you're reading a novel on your own, and purely for enjoyment, you're immersing yourself in the story; you want to *experience* the novel. If you are "into it," you'll of course pick up character names, plot details, and vocabulary words along the way; this will just come naturally. But you're not reading to get the facts; you're reading to understand, feel, and experience the story! It's a multidimensional kind of reading, really. You learn the story. You use your imagination to place yourself in the story. You empathize with the characters. You can't help but apply the situations of the novel to your life, and ask yourself how you would respond if you were placed in similar situations. That's how we read the Bible!

Second, the Bible as literature has an impact on how reading and studying it should affect our lives. You read billboards, box scores, and magazine covers, but they don't really have any lasting effect on your life. Literature, though, can *change people's lives*. It was a novel—*Phantastes*—that the great author C. S. Lewis said "baptized" his imagination; that book had a lasting effect on his life, work, and aims. Maybe you have been forever moved and affected by a poem or even a great film. It changed you because it touched your mind, your heart, and your emotions. We need to allow the Bible—God's Word as literature—to affect us in this way! We don't read and study it just to get the right answers, or to do our daily task for God. We read and study the Bible to be *changed* by it, in every way.

In essence, what I am saying here is that we need to read the Bible for *more than just propositions*. What is a proposition? It's a true statement—an assertion of a fact. We do learn facts from the Bible, it's true. We learn that Isaac was the son of

Abraham, and that Jesus was from Nazareth, and that King David was a descendant of Boaz and Ruth. But we read the Bible for so much more than answers to trivia (or Bible study) questions! We let the Bible in all its literary beauty *wash* over us. We allow it to affect our minds, hearts, and souls. We expect it to change us.

> "I've found that I walk closest with God when I intentionally study the Word, both on my own and with other guys my age. However, I've also found that being open in a Bible study with other Christian guys my age is one of the hardest things for me to do. Breaking the barriers in order to dive deeper into the Word is tough, but it is extremely worthwhile to me. It is through Bible study with other guys my age that I've learned the most about my relationship with God and what he wants me to do. Bible study with other Christian guys has built some of my closest friendships that are centered on faith and provided guys I know I can turn to over and over again when I need prayer and support."
> —Jamison Shimmel (student, Covenant College in Lookout Mountain, Georgia)

CONCLUSION

I've been arguing that the Bible is, among other things, *literature*. That has a bearing on the way we read it, study it, and are affected by it. But the Bible is not made up of just one type of literature; there are at least six different literary *genres* in the Bible. How to study the Bible with those specific genres in view will be the topic of the next chapter.

DISCUSSION QUESTIONS

WHAT DID WE JUST READ?

1. What does it mean to say that the Bible is literature? Does that mean we are putting it in the same "category" as any other novel we read?

2. Why isn't it disrespectful to God to study the Bible as a literary work?

3. How is literature meant to affect people?

SO WHAT?

1. What difference would it make to the way you studied the Bible if you paid more attention to its literary aspects?

2. How does the literary nature of the Bible teach us about God?

3. How can you put the things that you learned from this chapter into practice in Bible study?

5

EXPLORING BIBLICAL GENRES

"Old Testament passages are so diverse in genre, subject matter, purpose, and temporal setting that even more detailed reflection, direction, and guidance by means of example are needed, especially for the biblical-theological reading and preaching of challenging genres such as legal material, wisdom literature, and the covenant lawsuit pressed by the prophets."

—DENNIS JOHNSON[1]

HAVE YOU BEEN THERE?

James couldn't figure it out. He was a student leader in his youth group at church, and he had just finished an in-depth study of the book of Galatians with the rest of the leadership team. For the first time, James had begun to actually see the sentence structure of the apostle Paul's writings, as passages began to come alive to him in a new way.

The students had worked together diagramming sentences, and had learned tools to help them find the main point of each passage. Finally, Paul's writings were starting to take on some shape and organization in James' mind. Previously, they had seemed like long, run-on sentences filled with lots of deep-sounding theological thoughts! So, armed with a new set of tools for approaching the Bible, James moved on to study a different book on his own. Thinking it was time for a change, he opened a book from the Old Testament: Proverbs. It didn't take him too long to figure out that the approach he had taken when studying Galatians with his fellow student leaders wasn't quite working with Proverbs. The apostle Paul's sentences had been long, well-organized, and formed sections that seemed to hold together. Proverbs was a completely different story. It seemed like the proverbs came out in rapid-fire, without any discernible organization. James wondered whether he was doing something wrong. Was there a different way he should be studying Proverbs? Why weren't the methods he had used to study Galatians working with this very different book?

UNDERSTANDING BIBLICAL GENRES

While you may not have used the word "genre" recently (or ever) in conversation, you already have an instinctive understanding of literary genres, whether you know it or not. Think again about some of the things you might have read this past week. You drove past a billboard with a picture of happy people playing slot machines and waving money. You basically ignored it; you knew it was trying to get you to go to a casino! Maybe you read a textbook for school in the past few days. You read it, not purely for pleasure, but for the content contained in it. Maybe you even took some notes on it, or highlighted some important parts. If you like to bake, you may have diligently followed a recipe in a cookbook, being careful to use the right amounts of each ingredient. Some of you might have even gotten a "love letter" from a special someone. Now *that* you read very carefully! You probably read it more than once—poring over the words, giving them time to sink in.

Now, imagine that you read that love letter, the one we just mentioned, the way you read a textbook. Imagine reading it just for the "facts." You take notes on the key words, you try to identify a purpose statement, and you get out your highlighter to mark up the parts of the love note that seem the most important. I think you get my point: it would be ridiculous to read a love letter that way! You *instinctively* know that you are supposed to read a love letter differently than a school textbook, just as you read a billboard differently than you read a recipe for chocolate chip cookies. They belong to different *genres*. We are making unconscious decisions every day about how to *interpret and apply the things we read based on their literary genre.*

The Bible, as I've stated before, is literature. But it is not just one kind of literature! The Bible comes to us in at least six different major literary *genres* ("kinds" of literature). There is narrative (or story), prophecy, wisdom/poetry, apocalyptic writing, gospel, and epistle (or letter). Learning how to correctly understand and apply Bible passages within each of these major genres is essential for good Bible study. Just as you read a love letter differently than you read a textbook, so you read a letter from the apostle Paul differently than you read a story about King David. You apply them differently as well. Let's take a look at each of these biblical genres. We'll briefly describe some of their characteristics, and give some tips and tools for Bible study, interpretation, and application in each one.

OLD TESTAMENT NARRATIVE

"Old Testament narrative" is a fancy way of saying "story." The Bible, as you know, is absolutely full of stories! You grew up reading these; stories were most likely your first introduction to the Bible. Daniel and the lion's den. David and Goliath. Noah and the ark. Samson and Delilah. Adam and Eve. Stories, in fact, make up the majority of the Bible! If that's the case, then we have to figure out how to interpret and apply story passages from the Bible—especially in the context of Bible study. So, let's look at a few characteristics of Old Testament *narratives*, or stories.

Features

All stories, including biblical stories, are made up of some basic elements. There are main and supporting characters—the people of the story. There is always a plot—the action of the story. There is almost always some kind of conflict—the problem or tension in the story. Finally, there is usually a resolution—the way that the story gets "sorted out" at the end. Bible stories almost always have these same basic elements. The Old Testament writers were not writing to pass along propositions; they were telling stories! They were carefully crafting the plot, developing the characters, describing the conflict, and explaining the resolution. We need to read Bible stories as . . . stories—which of course contribute to our understanding of God, as he reveals himself to us through the *big* story of the whole Bible.

Studying Narrative Passages

Now, imagine for a moment that you are reading a novel for class at school. The teacher opens a discussion on chapters 1 and 2, which you have all read in preparation for the day's class. She begins by asking, "Can anyone tell me how many verbs the author used in the first sentence of the novel?" Confused, you and your classmates stare back at her blankly. She continues, "Well, then, did anyone note the number of times that the main character's name was used in the first chapter?" You look around at your friends in the class . . . and some of you begin to giggle . . .

You get the picture; that's not the way you read a novel! Some details are, of course, very important. But other details are not. What is important when you read and study a novel? The *story*. In class, you wouldn't waste time counting verbs or analyzing sentence structure too closely. You would focus on the characters, the conflict, and the development of the plot. You would discuss the artistic way the author weaves details together to make one seamless story. You would definitely spend time discussing the main point of the story!

That's the attitude we need to adopt when we read narrative portions of Scripture. We need to allow the *story* to speak. Here are just a few tips for you as you begin studying the stories of the Bible:

1. God is always the main character in the story. Ultimately, we need to remember that the Bible is God speaking to us. So, no matter how interesting (or confusing) the details of a particular story in the Bible, we know the ultimate purpose for its being there: to *reveal God to us*. A very safe question to ask of any narrative passage in the Bible is this: "What is this passage teaching us about *God*?"

2. In general, the narratives of the Bible are given to us to demonstrate *one big idea*—one lesson. This does not mean that there aren't dozens of "subthemes" in every Bible story; there certainly are! But we need to be careful to always ask, "Why is this story here?" or to put the

question a different way, "What is the *main thing* the author is trying to communicate by telling this story?" That leads us to the next point . . .

3. We need to remember that the stories of the Bible are told, and carefully crafted, by *human storytellers*. They are inspired by God, yes! But they are not inspired, remember, in some kind of weird, "possessed" way, in which the human authors were not conscious of what they were writing. This wasn't dictation by God! The writers of the Old Testament—Moses and Samuel, to name just two—carefully crafted their narratives in purposeful ways. This means that we should always ask this important question of any narrative text in the Bible: "Where do we see the 'waving hand' of the author?"[2] In other words, where is the author trying to get us to look? What is he trying to make sure we don't miss? The answer to this question leads, usually, to the main point of the story.

Applying Narrative Passages

Now we come to the trickiest part of studying the stories of the Bible: application. How do we rightly apply the narrative texts of the Bible to our lives today—in twenty-first-century North America? We almost can't even start talking about this without noting a few common mistakes that people make in applying Old Testament narrative passages. For example:

Moralizing. This is, basically, looking at a passage and making a merely *moral* application. If you're studying David and Goliath, for example, you might say, "David was brave, so we should be brave like David." Often what this mistake really consists of is taking a subtheme from the story and making it the main theme. It's true that we should be brave like David, but there's something more that we need to get from that story, especially in the context of the entire Bible.[3]

Spiritualizing. This is trying to get a spiritual meaning out of a story that was *never meant* to have that meaning! For example, to stick with David and Goliath, the giant becomes—not just a large Philistine man—but a "giant" in our lives (cancer, mean people, homework, terrorists). We *spiritualize* the story; Goliath becomes a spiritual force that we all need to battle in our lives, and we ignore the fact that he was a real person who fought against God's people long ago.

Allegorizing. This is a lot like spiritualizing, but it has to do with forcing an *allegory* out of something that wasn't intended to have an allegorical meaning. For example, years ago, some Bible teachers observed that Rahab (the prostitute in Jericho who helped the Israelite spies escape from the city undetected) hung a *scarlet thread* from the window of her house. The red color, for these teachers, came to symbolize the blood of Jesus! The colored thread became an allegory for the red blood of Jesus that saves sinners, just as the red thread indicated that Rahab should be saved when God's people invaded Jericho. That's making a pretty big jump that the story itself simply doesn't make!

You can probably fill in some other equally bizarre ways that people have tried to apply difficult Old Testament passages, so we'll stop there for now. We'll have an entire chapter on what is called "Biblical Theology," where we talk about reading the Bible as one big, connected story of God's redemption. That will, I hope, be very helpful in showing you how to rightly apply passages from the different biblical genres. But for now, here are a few helpful hints for rightly applying the story passages of the Bible:

1. **The *Example* principle.** While we should try to be careful to avoid "moralizing," as we mentioned before, we can't deny that a lot of Scripture passages—especially the stories of the Old Testament—are given to us to serve as *examples*. The apostle Paul actually says this. Speaking of the rebellion of God's people in the wilderness, he writes to the church at Corinth: "Now these things took place as examples for us, that we might not desire evil as they did" (1 Cor. 10:6). When we read and study Bible stories, we should learn from the examples of the characters—both good and bad!

2. **The *Ordinary Israelite* principle.** Basically, this principle of application means that it's usually a safe bet to find the *ordinary people of God* in the story and apply a passage the way they would have applied it. We are, most of us, "ordinary" people of God—Christians! So, when we read an Old Testament story, we should see how the events affected God's ordinary people in the original context. What were they doing? How did they react? What was God trying to teach them? The story of David and Goliath offers a great illustration for how this principle works. What were the ordinary Israelites doing in that story? They were *standing on the sidelines* while God's king—David—killed their great giant of an enemy for them. That realization should shape how we apply this passage to our lives; we should probably move from standing in the shoes of David to standing in the shoes of God's helpless people, who need a representative champion to fight the battle for them!

3. **The *God* principle.** We mentioned this briefly before, but it's worth saying one more time. The God of the Old Testament stories is the *same God* that we worship today, and know personally through Jesus Christ. God

has not changed! His character—his love and holiness and justice—stays the same. So, a good question for interpretation and application—at any point in the Bible—is this one: "What are we learning about God?"

4. **The *Big Story* principle.** We'll study this point much more in future chapters, but for now, we'll say just a couple of things. The Bible, remember, is one big story, with one ultimate author: God. It hangs together, and it develops along the way. This means that, when we read Old Testament stories, we need to *understand and apply them in light of the big story of the Bible.* It's a story that has its climax in the person and work of Jesus Christ. So, when we apply narrative passages, we should be asking, "How does this passage relate to—or point forward to—the climax of the big story?"

PROPHECY

Features

Today, a lot of people get prophecy wrong. Why? Because they think of prophecy in a very narrow way—usually as "predicting the future," or something like that. In reality, biblical prophecy is about much more than that! There are, of course, times when biblical prophets—or prophetic writings—predict, or point to, future events. But reducing the definition of prophecy to "predicting the future" means missing the full scope of what prophets were called and sent by God to do. So, what is prophecy?

Prophecy really has a pretty simple definition. It means *speaking God's Word to God's people.* That simplifies things, doesn't it? A prophet is someone who, in the days before Jesus Christ, was called to serve as a "mouthpiece" for God. Professor Grudem puts it this way: "The main function of the

Old Testament prophets was to be *messengers from God*, sent to speak to men and women with words from God. . . . They knew they were not speaking for themselves but for God who had sent them, and they spoke with his authority."[4]

The prophets spoke lots of different messages from God—words of hope, declarations of judgment, and, yes, sometimes future-looking predictions. While the definition of prophecy is quite simple, though, the prophecies that we read in the Bible are often far from easy to understand—as you probably know well, if you've ever tried to make your way through the book of Zechariah! So, first, what are some common features of biblical prophecy that we should be aware of in our study?

Vivid imagery. Biblical prophetic books are full of word pictures. Prophets tend to speak in cosmic terms; they make use of powerful metaphors and figures of speech. Often, illustrations are used to strengthen the prophet's point, and make God's Word really "stick" for the people. One example of this, which you'll find throughout the prophets, is the comparison of God's sinful people to a sexually unfaithful wife. Some prophets actually get very vivid and detailed as they discuss this metaphor! Why do prophetic writings do this? Because it's one thing to say to God's people, "You are sinful, rebellious, and unfaithful to your God." It's another thing to say, "You are a wife who keeps on committing adultery with lots of different men!" That metaphor strengthens the message; it helps God's people see even more clearly the reality of the truth God is speaking to them. This is something you will see often in prophecy.

Poetic language. As a genre, prophetic writings do have a lot in common with poetry. In fact, passages from prophetic books often read like poems; they come in two-line pairs, and can even be organized in extremely artistic ways. Sometimes, this means that prophecy can be a little hard to "organize" in our minds. Some chapters—in books such as Isaiah, Jeremiah, or Ezekiel—don't read like one of the well-crafted arguments of the apostle Paul: if A, then B, and so C . . . etc. Sometimes, this means that chapters in prophetic books can be "circular"—circling around and around on the same subject. Studying prophecy, and understanding it well, will mean taking seriously the poetic nature of a lot of what comes at us from the biblical prophets.

Judgment and wrath. It probably shouldn't be too surprising that what we find in many of the prophetic books is *God's judgment against sin.* After all, we know our own hearts, right? We know that we—like God's people in ancient Israel—often need to be reminded of our stubborn and rebellious hearts. We need to be reminded of God's Word, his goodness, and his grace. Still, the intense, often violent, descriptions of God's wrath against his people and other sinful nations can catch us off-guard sometimes. God gets angry at sin! This is probably most clear in the prophetic books. If we're going to study prophecy well, we're going to need to get ourselves ready to deal with lots of judgment. We're going to need to wrestle with the wrath of a holy God against human sin and rebellion, because it's all over the prophets.

Studying Prophecy

While Zechariah or Amos may not be the first two books you would choose for a Bible study at your school or church, I would encourage you to begin digging into some of the prophetic passages of Scripture that you may have avoided for a long time. God's Word is just that—God's Word. All of it. We have a lot to learn from the prophets in our culture today, because we often have more in common with God's people in ancient Israel than we like to admit. So, as you begin preparing to study books within the prophetic genre, here are a few important things to keep in mind:

Remember that prophecy is grounded in history. We've already mentioned the vivid imagery, poetic language, and intense judgment that characterizes a lot of prophetic writing in the Bible. It's easy, sometimes, to get lost in the midst of all that's going on in the prophets. Our eyes begin to glaze over, and we wonder what in the world we're supposed to do with the strange oracles that we're reading! We need to always remember that every prophetic word that we find in the Old Testament was written *to real people for a specific purpose.* We've got to remember that prophecy was grounded in history—in a real situation. And that historical context will always be to key to "getting it." The words of Micah, Amos, Isaiah, and Nahum were not just thrown up in the air randomly! They were given by God for his people to hear—at a specific time, in a specific place, and for a specific purpose. This simple realization will always be very helpful!

Move from prediction/completion to promise/fulfillment. This concept is a little complicated. You see, so often, using our "predicting the future" definition of prophecy, we think of the prophets as people who foretold future events that one day "came true." And, in some sense, there *is* some of that going on. Micah, for example, does "predict" that the Messiah for God's people will be born in the town of Bethlehem. Isaiah does point forward to a "suffering servant," who looks a lot like the suffering Jesus, who comes later on in the Bible story! Still, in general, the prophets tend to be a lot more about big promises—from God to his people—that are ultimately fulfilled in Jesus Christ. It's not always a "one-to-one" kind of completion. In fact, the amazing thing about the prophecies, as they relate to Jesus, is that Jesus fulfills them in ways that are *way more amazing* than God's people ever could have expected. A return to Israel, for example, is fulfilled in a far greater way in the hope we have, as Christians, in a future heavenly home. The hope for a new King David is fulfilled, not by a great human king, but by a *divine* king. The prophets are communicating God's promises to God's people. They're not simply making specific predictions.

Keep your eyes on God. Your safest bet, as you study prophetic passages, is to take care to stay very focused on God. We'll say the same thing several times over the course of this book, but that's because it's so important. God *does not change.* Yes, the way he chooses to work in the lives of his people changes slightly in the different periods of biblical history, but his holy character, power, love, and mercy are constant from all eternity. So keep your eyes on God when you're reading and studying prophecy. Pay attention to what *he* is doing. See what *he* is looking for from his people. Notice what *he* is angry about—or pleased with.

Applying Prophecy

While we live in a very different time from the Israelites who originally heard the words of Isaiah, Micah, Jeremiah, and Ezekiel, it is often amazing to me how applicable their messages are to us as Christians today. But this shouldn't really be too amazing! We are God's people now; they were God's people then. They were human beings then; we are human beings now. We have the same tendencies toward sin, and we often need rebuke and correction in similar ways. Here are just a few ways that the messages of the prophetic books tend to touch our lives today:

The prophetic writings call out religious hypocrisy. Over and over again, we see the prophets addressing the tendency of God's people to continue engaging in religious rituals, even as their moral and personal lives are out-of-control evil in the sight of God. It seems that a common problem for God's people was believing that sacrifices and religious "stuff" could keep them in a right relationship with God, even if their hearts were not completely given to him in worship. And isn't that our tendency too? Going to church and doing devotions become ways that we "pat ourselves on the back" spiritually, even as we pursue sin in other areas of our lives. The prophets' answer to that kind of attitude is very harsh, and very clear. They remind us of these words of God: "For I desire steadfast love and not sacrifice, the knowledge of God rather than burnt offerings" (Hosea 6:6). The prophets—and God himself—will not stand for religious hypocrisy. Religious rituals are never a substitute for a heart and life that are completely given over to the Savior.

They call for real repentance. Whether God's people live in the twenty-first century AD or the seventh century BC, the right response of sinful people to a holy God is always the same: genuine repentance of sin. That's exactly what the prophets call for from God's people again and again. They beg them, in God's name, to turn from their sin and return to God in faith, humility, and obedience. Even though we live centuries after these prophecies were first written, that message is alive and applicable to us today. Salvation comes as people truly repent (i.e., turn from their sin) and turn to a gracious God for mercy and salvation through Christ.

They point us to God's ultimate mercy. There's a lot of judgment language in the prophets. We've covered that briefly already. But, in almost every prophetic book, God's final and ultimate salvation plan is foreshadowed, or at least mentioned. The prophet Micah is a great example of this. There's plenty of judgment in the book of Micah, but God's judgment is not the last word! Listen to how Micah ends his prophecy:

> He will again have compassion on us;
>   he will tread our iniquities underfoot.
> You will cast all our sins
>   into the depths of the sea.
> You will show faithfulness to Jacob
>   and steadfast love to Abraham,
> as you have sworn to our fathers
>   from the days of old. (Micah 7:19–20)

Even a book filled with judgment ends with God's mercy! And that is applicable to us today. We *know* God's mercy; we've seen what it actually looks like, because we live in the days after the coming of Jesus. So we can apply passages like this one from Micah in the fullest way possible—by seeing their completion in the life, death, and resurrection of God's own Son.

WISDOM/POETRY

Other than maybe Old Testament narrative, there is probably no biblical genre that is so *fun* to read as wisdom/poetry. With vibrant imagery, unusual comparisons, and seemingly bizarre word pictures, this genre definitely captures our attention! Yet there is probably no biblical genre that young people find more difficult to understand and apply than this one. Consider, for example, this passage from a section of wisdom literature:

He who digs a pit will fall into it,
　and a serpent will bite him who breaks through a wall.
He who quarries stones is hurt by them,
　and he who splits logs is endangered by them.
If the iron is blunt, and one does not sharpen the edge,
　he must use more strength,
　but wisdom helps one to succeed.
If the serpent bites before it is charmed,
　there is no advantage to the charmer. (Eccl. 10:8–11)

There's a lot of interesting stuff there! Splitting logs. Quarrying stone. Charming serpents. But my guess is that if you read through that passage in your devotions this morning, or studied it in a small group at church, you've had a bit of trouble seeing how it applies to living a Christian life in the twenty-first century!

While the wisdom/poetry genre can be hard to understand—and even harder to apply—there are God-given depths of wisdom there that can and should speak to our lives today. It just takes a little (you guessed it!) hard working through the text. So, to help you become better equipped to study this genre, we'll look at a few of its key features.

Before we do that, though, let's clarify something. When we talk about the wisdom/poetry genre of the Bible, we are really talking about five specific books: Job, Psalms, Proverbs, Ecclesiastes, and Song of Solomon. These books, referred to by the ancient Israelite believers as "the Writings," are made up, overwhelmingly, of poetry. And what poetry it is! These books are some of the finest literary works ever assembled. Their authors were *masters* of language—true experts at putting words together in ways that are both beautiful and meaningful.

Features

Now, the minute I say the word "poetry," about 90 percent of you probably inwardly moan and groan, and your eyes roll

back into your head expecting a sudden onslaught of boredom.
But we need to realize that a good portion of God's inspired
Word does indeed come to us in poetic language. We won't
spend too long on this, but to really "get" the style, meaning,
and tone of the wisdom/poetry genre, you have to understand
a few things about Hebrew poetry.

Parallelism. Probably the most important aspect of Hebrew
poetry is its extremely common use of parallelism. It's really
a lot like what you might have heard called a "couplet" in
your study of other forms of poetry. Parallelism is two lines of
poetry that are meant to be together; they work in conjunc-
tion with one another, as a pair, to enhance what the writer
is trying to say. Here's one silly example of (non-biblical)
parallelism:

> My dog ate this morning;
> My dog ate *way too much* this morning.

It's pretty bad poetry, I'll admit! But you get the point. Two
lines, working together—in this case, to *enhance* or *amplify* the
meaning I'm trying to communicate. Under the general label
of "parallelism" in Hebrew poetry, there are a few different
subcategories.

Synthetic parallelism. In this kind of parallelism, the second
part completes the thought that was begun in the first part.
Here's one example of what this looks like in the Bible:

> There are those who are clean in their own eyes
> But are not washed of their filth. (Prov. 30:12)

Those two lines don't stand alone: the second line continues the
thought that was begun, and left incomplete, in the first line.

Amplified parallelism. This can also be called "synonymous parallelism," but the second line so often serves to *amplify* the point of the first line that I like to label it that way. That is, the second line says the same thing that was just said, but makes it even stronger. Here's an example of this:

> For he satisfies the longing soul,
>   and the hungry soul he fills with good things. (Ps. 107:9)

Do you see how the second line amplifies—and fills out—the point the author is making in the first line? The writer is talking about the same basic idea (God filling and satisfying human souls), but the repetition, with a slight change, makes the point "stick" even more. God doesn't just satisfy the longing soul; he does it by filling that soul with "good things."

Contrast parallelism. The more technical term for this is "antithetical parallelism." The second line in a pair like this *contrasts* with the first line. Here's one example:

> It is the glory of God to conceal things,
>   But the glory of kings is to search things out. (Prov. 25:2)

This is a pretty obvious figure of speech to recognize, which is good, because it's used all the time in wisdom/poetry, often to contrast the righteous person with the wicked person, or the way of God with the way of evil.

Now that you've gotten a little bit of a handle on parallelism, here are a few more features of Hebrew poetry that you should be aware of.

From time to time (especially in the psalms), you'll run across *acrostic* poetry. This is poetry that intentionally begins each line with a certain letter of the Hebrew alphabet. The most extensive example of an acrostic psalm is Psalm 119, in which the psalmist spends several verses for each letter in the Hebrew alphabet, all celebrating God's law. It's obviously a very long psalm!

Hebrew poetry tends to deal in *extremes*. While the stories of the Bible take us into the confusing details of everyday life, the poems and wisdom literature of the Bible present clear-cut alternatives. There are the righteous and the wicked, God's friends and God's enemies, right and wrong. Hebrew poetry often reminds us (many times through contrast parallelism) that, ultimately, there are two paths to choose from in life: the path toward God or the path away from him.

In a similar way to the prophecy genre, wisdom/poetry tends to gravitate toward vibrant *word pictures* and *metaphors* to communicate a point or idea. God's wrath is represented by thunder and lightning. God's enemies are depicted as wild animals—lions or dogs. When we take seriously the mental images these writings are trying to give us, we often understand their meaning even more clearly.

Studying and Applying Wisdom/Poetry

How are you doing? Too much poetry talk? Hang in there— we'll get a little more practical now. How do we rightly study the wisdom/poetry books of the Bible and interpret and apply them to our lives in the twenty-first century? Here are a few suggestions, building on our previous discussion, to get you started in your study of Job, Psalms, Proverbs, Ecclesiastes, and Song of Solomon:

Let the graphic images enrich your understanding of God and his salvation. Far too often, Christian life becomes boring. Worse, our view of salvation becomes boring. Worse still, God starts to become boring to us. This shouldn't be the case! Wisdom/poetry has the potential to remind us of the beauty of our God and the cosmic wonder of his salvation. Too often we get a little "bogged down" in the propositions of our faith. We recite well-known truths about God, such as "God is my Savior." The psalmist puts a picture to this:

> He drew me up from the pit of destruction,
> out of the miry bog,
> and set my feet upon a rock,
> making my steps secure.
> He put a new song in my mouth,
> a song of praise to our God. (Ps. 40:2–3)

That kind of psalm should be a huge boost to a faith that is in danger of getting boring! What does it *look like* for God to be our "Savior?" It looks like—spiritually—his lifting us out of a dirty pit of sin, setting us on a firm rock, and filling our hearts with the desire to sing to him at the top of our lungs. That's what salvation looks like . . . and sounds like. As we study the poetry of the Bible, we should be allowing our faith to be *illustrated* in the right biblical ways.

Let the extreme nature of this genre remind you of eternal clarity in the midst of temporal chaos. We talked just a bit ago about the extremes that this genre tends to present. There aren't too many "gray areas" in wisdom/poetry! There are the righteous and the wicked, the wrong path and the right path. This is something that is so hard to remember in everyday life, isn't it? Morality and obedience become difficult to discern sometimes. Do I see that movie? Should I say that word? Should I date that girl or guy? Wisdom/poetry brings us back to the eternal realities and the eternal clarity of the great, ultimate divide: the divide between those who follow God and those who don't. We need to remember, for example,

For the upright will inhabit the land,
    and those with integrity will remain in it,
but the wicked will be cut off from the land,
    and the treacherous will be rooted out of it. (Prov. 2:21–22)

When we are in danger of losing an absolute perspective on right and wrong, truth and lies, eternal life and eternal death, we should pick up the book of Proverbs! We'll be reminded that, in God's eyes, there are only two categories for every human being who has ever lived: righteous (in Christ) and wicked (apart from Christ). This genre can "jerk" us back into the eternal and clear realities of God's view of our world—and of our lives.

Let the beauty of wisdom/poetry inform you about God himself. Friends, the form of biblical poetry *itself* should be an encouragement to us about the character—and creativity—of our wonderful God! God, as he communicates his truth through human authors influenced by his divine inspiration, does so with *artistry* and *beauty.* God is not boring! He is creative. He loves artistic expression. Every good creative impulse—every good turn of phrase—is part of our being made in God's image. You remember the story of Job? When Job begins to question God's sovereign control over his life and situation, God could simply say, "Shut up, Job. I'm in charge." He would be completely justified in doing that. But he doesn't! He confronts Job sternly and forcefully, but in poetic language that reflects his intimate knowledge and careful design of nature. He questions him about lightning, thunder, stars, lions, mountain goats, wild oxen, and ostriches! God chooses to remind Job—through a detailed, beautiful speech about nature—of his sovereign control over every aspect of the world he has made, including Job's situation. And he could have just said "shut up!"

That is our God. An artist. Divinely creative. Using the words (that he himself created!) to speak to his people in ways that not only give them information, but also move their hearts and touch their emotions. The very existence of the wisdom/poetry genre in God's Word reveals to us God's amazing personality, character, creativity, and love.

APOCALYPTIC WRITING

Crack open the book of Revelation, and it doesn't take too long to realize that we are in a pretty different kind of place. Dragons. Strange scenes from heaven. Beasts with horns. The genre of apocalyptic literature is definitely a foreign genre; there are some weird things going on!

But let me suggest to you—especially you young people—that we're not actually as poorly equipped to engage with and study apocalyptic literature in the Bible as you might think. Consider the movies that are popular today, and the books that you and your friends like to read. When I was younger, it was *The Matrix* trilogy. Now we've seen *Avatar,* as well as several other popular films in the science fiction genre. We love weird, "other-worldly" literature, stories, and entertainment. Maybe the book of Revelation—and the apocalyptic genre—is not as bizarre as we think. We are actually quite comfortable with weird stuff!

When we say "apocalyptic literature," we are of course mainly referring to the book of Revelation. That is definitely one of the most difficult books in the Bible to interpret; many of you have probably been thrown for a loop trying to understand it. But Revelation is not the only book in the Bible that contains this genre. Many of the prophets—Zechariah and Daniel, for example—have portions that are clearly apocalyptic. So, to help you in your study of this genre of Scripture, we'll look at some of its features, and then discuss some helpful approaches for interpreting it.

Features

Cosmic scope. It doesn't take too long, when reading the book of Revelation, to discover that the events and themes described almost always center on the activity of God and have effects that span the entire world. Apocalyptic literature is usually *cosmic* in its scope. It doesn't waste time with trivial details; the discussion and the events are global, eternal, and all-important. Consider, for example, Revelation 8. We discover that seven angels are preparing to blow trumpets. Here's what we read about the first angel: "The first angel blew his trumpet, and there followed hail and fire, mixed with blood, and these were thrown upon the earth. And a third of the earth was burned up, and a third of the trees were burned up, and all green grass was burned up" (v. 7).

What is described in Revelation 8 is not something that affects a certain people group or a specific geographical area. The scope is cosmic! Hail, fire, and blood are thrown down upon the earth, and *one third* of the earth is burned up. This is a massive event that is being described, not a localized, small occurrence.

Figurative language. While many godly and wise biblical scholars disagree on what parts of Revelation are to be taken literally and what parts are to be taken figuratively (or spiritually), almost everyone agrees that, to some extent, figurative language is used in the book of Revelation. Even interpreters who choose to take numbers and times literally (such as the 144,000 people in Revelation 14, for example) agree that the following verses make use of some figures of speech: "Then I heard a loud voice from the temple telling the seven angels,

'Go and pour out on the earth the seven bowls of the wrath of God'" (Rev. 16:1). Does that mean that there are angels with *literal* bowls—made out of wood, metal, or glass—waiting in heaven to pour out some kind of "liquid" wrath on the earth? Of course not. The "bowls" are a figurative way of describing the outpouring of God's anger against sin.

Even in less obviously figurative passages, though, it seems that biblical writers of apocalyptic literature are using the *language and descriptions of their times to attempt to describe cosmic heavenly realities*. Think about it. If people from ancient Israel saw a helicopter, how would they describe it? They would probably speak in terms of a giant, loud, flying monster-insect, right? It's the same way for biblical writers who were exposed to the heavenly realities of God and his work in the world. It would be the same way for us today if we were to get a glimpse "behind the scenes" in the throne room of God. We wouldn't know how to put into words the glories of heaven and the magnificent holiness of God! We'd try, though. We'd talk about "fire," and "gold," and "bright light," but none of it would really describe what we had really seen. We don't have the *categories* or *language* to fully describe it. In the same way, biblical writers of apocalyptic literature—such as John, the author of Revelation—used the best words they could to describe their visions of heavenly things, which are beyond human expression.

Future orientation. We can't deny that much of apocalyptic literature does have a future orientation. Take the book of Revelation, again, as an example. While there is endless debate about whether certain events have happened already, will happen in the future, or are happening now in a figurative sense, there are some parts of Revelation that will certainly occur in the future. Take this passage, for example:

Then I saw a new heaven and a new earth, for the first heaven and the first earth had passed away, and the sea was no more. And I saw the holy city, new Jerusalem, coming down out of heaven from God, prepared as a bride adorned for her husband. (Rev. 21:1–2)

This is a vision of the future—a glimpse of what is coming for God's people. Whether a biblical scholar believes that Satan will be "bound" in the future or has already been "spiritually bound" by Jesus' death and resurrection, he or she has to agree that the new heaven and new earth have not yet come. And, since we're still walking around on it, the "first earth" has not yet passed away! Revelation—this apocalyptic book—gives us a cosmic vision of the future. It tells us where everything is ultimately and finally *headed*. This earth is racing toward the day when God will create a new heaven and new earth, and all his people will come to be with him forever—made perfect as a beautiful bride.

Studying and Applying Apocalyptic Writing

Whether or not your next youth Bible study will be in the book of Revelation, you should plan to study it at some point! And you need to be equipped to handle other apocalyptic passages of Scripture with understanding too, so that you know how to let God's Word affect your life. So, here are a few words of instruction for you as you study, interpret, and apply Bible passages from this genre:

Don't get lost in debate. In some ways, this may be the most important guideline for apocalyptic literature. The greatest danger you'll face when studying this genre is that—in your arguments and debates about meaning—you'll actually miss the main point that the passage is there to teach us! We so easily get sidetracked on subpoints that we forget the main point. Imagine that you're studying Revelation 7 with some friends from church. It begins with a vision of 144,000 people, "sealed from every tribe of the sons of Israel" (v. 4). You begin to discuss this. One person insists that this is a literal number. Someone else argues that this is a figurative picture of what is simply a very large group of people. Another person wants to get into what this means for the people in the world today who are ethnically Jewish.

Now, I'm not saying this debate is completely unimportant. So long as Scripture includes passages like this, we need to study every detail carefully and arrive at the most reasonable conclusion about their meaning. Some people simplify it too much, and just say, "Jesus wins; what else matters?" That betrays an attitude that doesn't take the biblical text seriously enough! But, if you get too bogged down in the 144,000 (to stick with the example above), you miss what happens in the rest of the chapter. When we read on, we find that "a great multitude" joins the 144,000. Who are these people? They are those who "have washed their robes and made them white in the blood of the Lamb" (Rev. 7:14). This passage isn't so much meant to get us focused on *how many* people are in this gathering (although it's definitely a large number). This passage is meant to get us focused on *how these people got there!* It's about JESUS. It's all about the huge gathering of redeemed people that come together because of his saving blood. Friends, when you're studying apocalyptic literature, don't get lost in the debate so much that you miss the main point.

Find God and his people. In the tough passages of apocalyptic literature, it is important to identify the main characters that we always need to locate: God and his people. Just as in the prophetic genre, it's always good in apocalyptic passages to be

EXPLORING BIBLICAL GENRES

asking, "What is this teaching us about *God*?" The follow-up question is, "What does this teach us about human beings and their appropriate response to God?" Those two basic questions will help keep you grounded, because even the most obscure apocalyptic passages come back to the character of God and the right response of his redeemed people—whether or not dragons and scorpions are involved!

Jesus is the point. We'll go into this in a lot more detail in the next chapter, but in apocalyptic literature (as in the entire Bible), we need to be always finding *Jesus.* If the Bible is really about Jesus (and Jesus says it is), then Jesus really is the point. I demonstrated how that worked just a bit ago with Revelation 7 and the 144,000 people. The point of that passage was not to get us hung up on a number; the point was to direct our attention to Jesus, whose blood creates a huge gathering of people who rejoice together at his salvation. Here's one more example of how this could play out in Bible study. Take a quick read of Revelation 13:1–10:

> And I saw a beast rising out of the sea, with ten horns and seven heads, with ten diadems on its horns and blasphemous names on its heads. And the beast that I saw was like a leopard; its feet were like a bear's, and its mouth was like a lion's mouth. And to it the dragon gave his power and his throne and great authority. One of its heads seemed to have a mortal wound, but its mortal wound was healed, and the whole earth marveled as they followed the beast. And they worshiped the dragon, for he had given his authority to the beast, and they worshiped the beast, saying, "Who is like the beast, and who can fight against it?"
>
> And the beast was given a mouth uttering haughty and blasphemous words, and it was allowed to exercise authority for forty-two months. It opened its mouth to utter blasphemies

against God, blaspheming his name and his dwelling, that is, those who dwell in heaven. Also it was allowed to make war on the saints and to conquer them. And authority was given it over every tribe and people and language and nation, and all who dwell on earth will worship it, everyone whose name has not been written before the foundation of the world in the book of life of the Lamb who was slain. If anyone has an ear, let him hear:

> If anyone is to be taken captive,
>   to captivity he goes;
> if anyone is to be slain with the sword,
>   with the sword must he be slain.

Here is a call for the endurance and faith of the saints.

Now, if you're not careful, what will you focus on in this passage? The *beast*, right? Who is this beast? Is he a person? A spiritual being? When will he come? How will he come? Will we recognize him? Now, those are not bad questions. We need to ask those questions of the text, and we need to study how this beast is described; he certainly takes up a good part of this passage! But if we ask where *Jesus* is, we find that the answer is the most important part of the passage. Who worships this evil beast? Everyone *except* those whose names have been written in the "book of life of the Lamb who was slain" (Rev. 13:8). So, no matter who this beast is, those who belong to Jesus will be *safe* from his influence. The point for us as we read this passage is not to *figure out the identity of the beast*. It's to *make sure we're in Jesus Christ the Savior*. No matter who this beast is, the application is the same: find safety in Jesus!

Future orientation always has present moral implications. There is a tendency, when you're studying apocalyptic literature, to get so focused on future events that you miss the very practical application of what this genre is teaching. In Revelation, for example, you'll be looking forward a lot—forward to the new heaven and new earth, and to the final return of Christ. But the application of those things is *always* about righteous living *now* in Christ! Think back to that passage we just looked at from Revelation 13. It talks about the beast, and the destruction and damage he will cause on the earth. But how does the passage end? With a very real and practical application: "Here is a call for the endurance and faith of the saints" (Rev. 13:10). Cosmic scope. Future orientation. A huge vision of trouble, struggle, and the ultimate victory of Christ. What does the application boil down to? Endurance and faith *now*. Day by day. Apocalyptic literature should have a huge impact on how we view the future, yes, but it should have an even greater impact on how we live today for Jesus Christ.

GOSPEL

There's been a lot of debate among Bible scholars about what the gospel genre really is. Is it narrative, in the same category as the stories of the Old Testament? Is it similar to ancient hero stories, that describe in almost mythical terms the accomplishments and exploits of an amazing man or woman? It's definitely a complex genre! It contains stories, sermons, some poetry, and of course parables—which could be considered a genre all to themselves. So, what are the gospels all about? How do we wrap our minds around this genre?

In a word, the gospels are all about a person: Jesus. That's the most important thing you need to know! Are they a genre all their own? Well, in the sense that they are completely focused on the person of Jesus—his character, identity, and actions—then, yes. They are absolutely unique. But they are not so foreign a genre that the rules of literature somehow don't apply to them. The gospels, like other writings in the Bible, are telling a story. Their story is all about Jesus, of course, but the writers carefully chose their words and crafted their sentences in order to tell the story in a specific way. And, while the gospel writers were all writing the story of Jesus, they wrote with slightly different purposes—and for slightly different audiences as well. Consider, for example, the different purposes that the gospel writers Luke and John had in mind:

First, John:

> Now Jesus did many other signs in the presence of the disciples, which are not written in this book; but these are written so that you may believe that Jesus is the Christ, the Son of God, and that by believing you may have life in his name. (John 20:30–31)

Whatever John was up to along the way as he wrote his gospel, we know that his primary purpose was that the readers of this gospel would *believe* that Jesus really is the Son of God, and that they therefore would have *life* in his name. John was telling the story of Jesus, yes, but he was doing it for a very specific purpose. He wanted to bring about belief, and therefore, life.

Second, listen to Luke:

> Inasmuch as many have undertaken to compile a narrative of the things that have been accomplished among us, just as those who from the beginning were eyewitnesses and ministers of the word have delivered them to us, it seemed good to me also, having followed all things closely for some time past, to write an orderly account for you, most excellent Theophilus, that you may have certainty concerning the things you have been taught. (Luke 1:1–4)

Luke was writing his gospel about the same person John was: Jesus. But he had a slightly different purpose than John. He was writing for a man—Theophilus—and he was trying to write an "orderly account" of the life of Jesus, in order to bring this man "certainty" about the teachings he'd heard about Jesus. Luke's gospel, we can assume, will have a slightly different "feel" than John's gospel. John was trying to bring *belief and life*; Luke was trying to bring *certainty*.

So, with this introduction in mind, let's turn to a few key features of each gospel. My hope is that these will help prepare you to study them, and to apply them powerfully to your lives!

Features of Matthew

Matthew is usually considered the most "Jewish" of the four gospels. What do I mean by that? I mean that Matthew was—more than any other gospel writer—concerned with Jesus as *the promised Jewish Messiah*. As the one who had come to fulfill all the promises God made to Israel throughout the entire Old Testament. The way Matthew began his gospel, then, is not too surprising: he started with a genealogy. As Matthew opened the story of Jesus' life, deeds, death, and resurrection, he wanted to show where Jesus came from, historically and ethnically. Jesus comes (humanly speaking) from the line of Abraham, Isaac, Jacob, and David. He is descended from the royal Jewish line of kings! Matthew wanted to show us Jesus, but more specifically, he wanted to show us the Jesus who is the promised eternal king of God's people—descended from David, and chosen by God to rule over his people forever.

If there's one theme that emerges as central to the gospel of Matthew, it's probably the theme of *authority*. Beginning with Jesus' genealogy helps Matthew establish his authority as the kingly Messiah of God's people. After this, there are several stops along the way where Matthew seems to work hard to show us the full divine authority of Jesus. At the famous Sermon on the Mount, for example, Jesus functions as the authoritative teacher and interpreter of God's Word. Listen to what Matthew says when Jesus finishes this famous sermon: "The crowds were astonished at his teaching, for he was teaching them as one who had authority, and not as their scribes" (Matt. 7:28–29).

Matthew ends, too, with another focus on Jesus' authority. After the resurrection, as Jesus prepares to send his disciples out into the world with the message of salvation through him, here's what he tells them:

> All authority in heaven and on earth has been given to me. Go therefore and make disciples of all nations, baptizing them in the name of the Father and of the Son and of the Holy Spirit, teaching them to observe all that I have commanded you. And behold, I am with you always, to the end of the age. (Matt. 28:18–20)

As Matthew's story of Jesus draws to a close, we are left with a picture of the great Messiah who has had all authority given to him. He is sending out his disciples to tell the world about his reign, his authority, and his Word. Matthew is showing his readers that the ultimate King of God's people has actually come—and his name is Jesus.

Features of Mark

Imagine that your little brother comes sprinting into your house, panting from running several blocks, extremely eager to tell you about the amazing thing he just saw at the park. That's how Mark's gospel comes out. Breathless. Fast-paced. Leaving out all unnecessary details and getting straight to the facts. One of Mark's favorite words must have been "immediately." It appears time after time to transition from section to section in his gospel. The reader of Mark gets the feeling that he was breathlessly gushing information about something extremely important, and he didn't want to get bogged down by anything!

Because Mark is the shortest gospel, most people think that it was also the earliest gospel—the first one written. John Mark, the writer, probably got a lot of his firsthand information from the apostle Peter. There is also some good evidence that parts of the other gospels are based on the events and descriptions that Mark recorded in his gospel.

One major theme that comes out in the gospel of Mark is the unbelief, fear, and even stupidity of the disciples. They just don't seem to "get" Jesus—his identity, purpose, or goals. Over and over again, Mark shows us how even Jesus' closest disciples fail to grasp what Jesus is really all about. We won't go into a lot of detail here about ancient manuscript evaluation, but a lot of scholars believe that the original version of the gospel of Mark ended at 16:8. If that's the case, Mark's emphasis of the unbelief and fear of the disciples comes through even more clearly. Jesus, after telling his disciples multiple times during his life that he will die and then rise from the dead, has just done exactly those things. The disciples show up at the tomb, and Jesus isn't there. So they assume that he has risen, right? Nope. An angel even shows up to *tell* them he has risen. They respond with faith and joy, right? Nope. Here's how Mark apparently chose to conclude his gospel: "And they went out and fled from the tomb, for trembling and astonishment had seized them, and they said nothing to anyone, for they were afraid" (Mark 16:8).

Mark's gospel ends with the disciples still not quite "getting" what Jesus was all about. That he came to die for sins, and then to rise again from the dead in order to conquer death forever. It's not until later that they finally get it and start telling others about it!

Features of Luke and Acts

The comparison earlier in this section has hopefully given you a bit of a "feel" for the gospel of Luke already. The book was written (obviously) by Luke, who was a physician by profession, and was writing in order to present an "orderly" account of the life, teaching, and work of Jesus to a man named Theophilus. Luke also wrote the book of Acts—the continuation of the story that he began in his gospel. To get a good sense of the whole story, it would probably be helpful for us to make a practice of reading Luke and Acts together, since Luke intended the book of Acts to carry on his account for Theophilus.

If we've labeled Matthew the most "Jewish" gospel—presenting Jesus as the Jewish Messiah for God's people—we can probably call Luke the most "Gentile" gospel. Luke's emphasis, throughout the parables and accounts of Jesus that he chooses to include, seems to be on Jesus as the Savior for *all kinds of people*. Gentiles and Jews. Clean and unclean. Rich and poor. Pharisees and "sinners." There are times, too, when Luke seems to take extra time to explain certain Jewish customs to his readers—something that Matthew, writing to a more Jewish audience, wouldn't have had to do.

One clear place where we find Luke's emphasis on the salvation Jesus offers to *all* kinds of people is in chapter 15, which contains the well-known parable of the prodigal son. The chapter describes the situation this way:

> Now the tax collectors and sinners were all drawing near to hear him. And the Pharisees and the scribes grumbled, saying, "This man receives sinners and eats with them." So he told them this parable . . . (Luke 15:1–3)

The chapter begins with a confrontation: Jesus versus the Pharisees (the strictest and most disciplined religious leaders of his day). They take issue with his interaction with and care for "sinners"—people who were both ritually and morally unclean. Jesus responds by telling them three parables: the lost sheep, the lost coin, and the lost son (or "prodigal" son). In each of the first two parables, there is a certain rhythm: something is *lost*, something is *found*, and then there is great *joy*. In the parable of the prodigal son, however, the pattern changes! The son is *lost*, the son is *found*, there is great *joy* . . . but then, something else happens. There is *grumbling*—from the older son of the gracious father. The chapter began with the Pharisees grumbling; Jesus is representing them in the parable by the character of the older son. Luke's point? Jesus is *all about saving lost people*—Jews, Gentiles, clean, dirty, rich, and poor. The Pharisees just couldn't get that!

Features of John

The gospel of John is different from the other three gospels in many ways. In fact, the other three—Matthew, Mark, and Luke—are often referred to as the *synoptic* gospels. Synoptic means "similar" or "same." They all seem to rely on the same eyewitness accounts of Jesus' life, probably from Peter, and they most likely build on the earliest gospel written, which was probably Mark. Because of this, the first three gospels have a lot in common. They tell many of the same parables and stories, even though they were written (as we've seen) with slightly different purposes and emphases.

John, though, was coming from a completely different direction. He wrote for the purpose of *belief*; we've talked about that. And, in trying to foster belief in his readers, he relied on a different set of stories and a different set of teachings from the ones used in the other gospels. Here are a few key differences between John's gospel and the synoptic gospels:

*John starts with **theology**.* Remember how Matthew started his gospel? With a genealogy—pointing his readers to Jesus' identity as the King of the Jews, the promised Messiah. John's gospel begins in a very different way. It goes back, not to the beginning of the Jewish people, but to the very beginning of time. John starts with the *eternal identity* of Jesus as the second person of the Godhead. You remember, I'm sure, the well-known beginning of John's gospel:

> In the beginning was the Word, and the Word was with God, and the Word was God. He was in the beginning with God. All things were made through him, and without him was not any thing made that was made. (John 1:1–3)

Before the apostle told his readers anything that Jesus *did*, he wanted them to be absolutely clear about who Jesus *is*. He was writing about the eternally existent, all-powerful co-Creator of the entire universe! John started with theology; he was "up front" about the identity of the man whose story he was going to write. This Jesus . . . is *God*.

*John describes **signs**, rather than miracles or healings.* Keeping in line with this focus on theology, the gospel of John tends to describe Jesus' amazing works not as "miracles" or "healings," but as *signs*. After Jesus changes water into wine at a wedding in Cana, for example, John summarizes the event with these words: "This, the first of his signs, Jesus did at Cana in Galilee, and manifested his glory" (John 2:11). Why does John label Jesus' miracles in this way? Because in this gospel, their primary function is to direct people's attention to the true identity of Jesus. His miracles are not just fun and amazing feats of strength! They are intentional and carefully placed *signs* that Jesus uses to show people *who he is*. Jesus isn't just about miracles for the sake of the miracles. He is all about pointing people to his true identity, and to personal belief in him. It's that belief that leads to eternal life.

*John seems to write for a more **global** audience.* Because of the two characteristics of the gospel of John described above, it does seem that John was writing for a more *global* audience than any of the other gospel writers. Mark seems to have been intent on recording facts—quickly and breathlessly. Matthew seems to have written for Jews. Luke wrote for Theophilus, but also for Gentiles generally. John, though, seems to have had the *entire world* in mind as he wrote about Jesus. This Jesus is the Savior of the entire world! That's why John started all the way back at creation—because Jesus was there. He was writing not just about the Jewish Savior, but about the Savior of all people, in every place, for all time. It's this "global scope" of John's gospel that makes it a wonderful first book for non-Christians to read; John wanted to show them Jesus as the eternal Son of God, and help them believe in *him*.

EPISTLE

Are you still with me? It's been a long ride, I know, going through all six of the main genres that we find in the Bible! Now, finally, we come to the one you're probably most familiar with, especially in the context of Bible study: the epistle.

The word "epistle" just means "letter." The epistles in the Bible are letters, written by apostles (people who had face-to-face interactions with Jesus), to teach early believers in Jesus about the truths of the gospel and about life as followers of Christ. Most people divide the epistles into three basic types:

Church epistles. These are letters written by the apostle Paul to specific congregations. This category consists of Romans,

1 Corinthians, 2 Corinthians, Galatians, Ephesians, Philippians, Colossians, 1 Thessalonians, 2 Thessalonians, and Philemon.

Pastoral epistles. These are letters written by the apostle Paul to specific early church leaders or pastors. This category consists of 1 Timothy, 2 Timothy, and Titus.

General epistles. This is just a basic label given to the rest of the letters in the New Testament, which were written by various authors, and generally to wider audiences. The general epistles consist of Hebrews, James, 1 Peter, 2 Peter, 1 John, 2 John, 3 John, and Jude.

Understanding and Applying Epistles

In many ways, the epistles of the Bible are the easiest books to read, understand clearly, and apply directly to our situation today as Christians. They were written to churches; we are part of churches. They were written after the death, resurrection, and ascension of Jesus; we still live in this same period of "salvation history." Early Christians had problems and struggles as they tried to live for Jesus; we have problems and difficulties too! These are all reasons why a majority of the Bible studies you've been involved in have probably focused on one of the epistles.

However, while it's true that the letters of the New Testament are the most easily understandable and applicable parts of Scripture to us as Christians today, it will still be important to keep a few general principles in mind as we study them:

Epistles were written to specific churches at specific times. This principle means that the very first thing we always need to do when we're studying a letter in the Bible is to consider its *context.* Who wrote it? To whom was it written? *Why* was it written? We always need to figure out what the letter meant to its original readers in

110

the original historical context. Many pastors and scholars have pointed out that a passage in the Bible cannot mean something that it *never meant*! Paying careful attention to the specific context of New Testament epistles will save us from a multitude of wrong interpretations and misunderstandings of the text.

Epistles were written as entire letters. We often study the Bible, especially in our personal devotions, in very small chunks. We take one verse—from the book of Romans, for example—and read it as our "thought for the day." What's the problem with this approach? The apostle Paul didn't write a verse at a time to the church in Rome. He wrote an *entire letter*. Not only that, but when a letter was received it was most likely read out loud—all at one time—to the church. Every verse we read, and every verse we study in a Bible study group, comes as part of a larger whole; in this case, verses are sentences that are part of letters. Remember that chapter and verse divisions aren't inspired! They came later. When the epistles were originally written, they showed up at the door of churches as long letters. They were read as letters to the people of the church.

Epistles were written to people living after Christ's ascension. While we need to take care to evaluate the context of each New Testament epistle, and acknowledge that these are actually letters, we can rightly apply much of what each letter says *directly* to our situation today. We can do this in a way that we can't with some parts of the Old Testament! Why is this? It's because we live during the *same period in salvation history* as the recipients of Paul's, Peter's, and John's letters. Yes, we live thousands of years after them. But, when it comes to God's salvation plan, we're in the same "age." Christ has come, died, risen, and ascended into heaven. We—like the ancient Christians of Ephesus—are waiting for the second coming of Jesus. We're all in the same spot, at least when it comes to salvation history—post-ascension and pre–second coming. So, when we hear Paul giving instructions to Christians in Galatia, we can generally apply those instructions directly to our lives as Christians. This is different from, for example, passages in the Old Testament in which God's people are commanded to kill their enemies! We live in a different age than Old Testament believers; we don't wage literal war against people who don't love God. But when we read Paul's warnings against false teachers who distort the gospel of grace, for example, we can apply his words directly to our situation today!

> "My favorite story is of a kid named Brandon who was in a small group I led. He was a charismatic kid with tons of charm, but he was arrogant too. He came from a broken home and was a new believer. Over the course of two years I saw him wrestle with the Word, argue with it, try to obey it, rebel against it, but overall I saw a steady upward crawl in sanctification. Today he is a youth pastor in Missouri and a passionate Bible teacher. Many of the kids from that youth group have walked away from the Lord in one way or another, but he remains passionate about seeking to serve Jesus. I credit the work of the Word in his life."
> —Barnabas Piper (former youth leader, College Church in Wheaton, Illinois)

DIFFERENT GENRES, ONE STORY

So we've made it through every major biblical genre. It's been a 30,000-foot look at them—we haven't gone into a lot of detail. But hopefully you've gotten at least a sense of some of the distinctive features of each of the six genres, as well as some starting tips and principles about how you should interpret them and apply them in the context of Bible study.

The amazing thing about the Bible, though, is that while it contains many different genres of writing, there is still one main story—one central plot—that holds the entire thing together. That big story, and what it means for Bible study, will be the subject of the next couple of chapters.

DISCUSSION QUESTIONS

WHAT DID WE JUST READ?

1. What are the six main literary genres found in the Bible?

2. What are some mistakes that we make in applying a passage from, for example, the Old Testament narrative genre?

3. Why is an understanding of different biblical genres so important for Bible study?

4. How do even the four gospels differ from one another?

SO WHAT?

1. What book is your pastor or youth pastor preaching from right now? How does the genre of that book impact that way it should be understood and applied?

2. How does the existence of different genres in the Bible enrich our knowledge and understanding of God?

3. What steps can you take, in Bible study, to both recognize and understand the genre of the book you're studying?

6

THE BIBLE IS ONE STORY

"Biblical theology forms an organic whole. This means not only that one can approach any part of the subject by beginning at any other point of the subject (though some vantage points are certainly more helpful than others), but that to treat some element of biblical theology as if it existed in splendid isolation seriously distorts the whole picture."

—D. A. CARSON[1]

HAVE YOU BEEN THERE?

Esther had grown up loving the stories of the Bible. She could recall most of the well-known ones by memory—almost verse by verse! Moses and the parting of the Red Sea. David and Goliath. Daniel and the lion's den. The miracles of Jesus, and his death and resurrection. The experiences and journeys of the apostle Paul in the book of Acts. Because of these stories, the Bible had always been very interesting to Esther. To her, it contained some of the best literature that had ever been written, and some of the most engaging narrative accounts she had ever encountered. One day, while sitting in church, she heard her pastor refer to the "story" of the Bible. At first she thought she had heard him wrong, but then he repeated himself: "story" . . . singular. What could that mean? Esther had always known that the Bible contained lots of engaging stories about God's people throughout the years, but was there really one *main* story that the Bible was telling? That was hard to believe. What did Moses have to do with David anyway? What did Daniel and the lion's den have to do with the missionary journeys of Paul? If the Bible was really just one story, she certainly didn't see it!

ONE STORY?

As Jamal Malik's interesting and difficult life develops, he has no idea what is ultimately in store for him. Orphaned at a young age, barely escaping death several times, faced with bullying and violence from local gangs, and losing the one girl he loves—Jamal has a sad story and a tough life! Yet, as the plot of the movie *Slumdog Millionaire* unfolds, we begin to see how all Jamal's experiences, even the difficult ones, contribute to his amazing ability to answer question after question correctly on the Indian version of the game show "Who Wants to Be a Millionaire?" What seem to be disconnected events all come together in the perfect way for Jamal; that is the beauty and wonder of the story.

Sometimes, as we read the Bible, it can seem a bit like the life of Jamal Malik. Disconnected stories. Random events. We've talked a lot already about the vastly differing genres of writing contained in the Bible. Is there any unifying theme?

Does anything ultimately bring this volume together, other than the fact that someone, somewhere, decided to put these sixty-six books in the same binding?

Before we get into the theology behind this question, consider for a moment the way the Bible begins and ends—with the books of Genesis and Revelation. To summarize briefly, the Bible begins in a garden—the garden of Eden. There are four rivers that run through this garden, and a tree, called the Tree of Life, that sits right in the middle (Gen. 2:9). Now, think with me about the way the Bible wraps up in the book of Revelation—in the very last chapter. Here's what we find there:

> Then the angel showed me the river of the water of life, bright as crystal, flowing from the throne of God and of the Lamb through the middle of the street of the city; also, on either side of the river, the tree of life with its twelve kinds of fruit, yielding its fruit each month. (Rev. 22:1–2)

Now, the picture isn't identical (the Bible starts in a garden and ends in a city), but we do see some striking similarities between the way the Bible begins and the way it ends, don't we? There's a river—at the beginning, and at the end. And the Tree of Life shows up again in Revelation, a vision of the end. We haven't heard from this tree since the earliest chapters of Genesis! We're on to something here. The book of Genesis, written more than a thousand years before the book of Revelation, is talking about some of the same themes and images that we find at the very end of the Bible. There are hints that the book of Revelation is concluding the *same story* that began in the book of Genesis!

But what is it that brings this story together? For Jamal, there was a game show—an opportunity for him to draw his life experiences together in his astonishing ability to answer every question correctly. What about the Bible? If it really is

117

one story that begins in Genesis and ends in Revelation, then what is it all about? What is the center?

JESUS: THE STORY'S CENTER

Thankfully, we have the witness of the Son of God himself—Jesus—to give us some help here! What is the story of the Bible all about? What is the center of it? Jesus says, "I am!" According to Jesus, he is the center and the climax of the entire story of the Bible—the epicenter of God's redemptive work in the world he created. The entire story hinges on his life, death, and resurrection.

John 5

One place we see Jesus making this point very clearly is in John 5, in the midst of a heated exchange with his regular opponents, the Pharisees. The Pharisees, as you may know, were the strictest group of Jewish teachers and leaders during the time of Jesus. They were disciplined and learned in the law, and they—or at least many of them—knew the Old Testament Scriptures completely by heart! But they had missed an extremely important point about the witness of the Law and the Prophets: that they all pointed to Jesus as the great Messiah of God's people. Jesus tells them as much: "You search the Scriptures because you think that in them you have eternal life; and it is they that bear witness about me, yet you refuse to come to me that you may have life" (John 5:39–40).

That is a huge statement that Jesus makes to these religious leaders! Did you catch the implications of what he's saying? The Scriptures (Genesis to Malachi) bear witness about *him*. "It's all about *me*," Jesus is telling them. The Law, the Prophets, the Writings—they all point forward to one person who will fulfill all the promises of God to his people. For the Pharisees, this means that as well as they know the Scriptures, they don't really *understand* them unless they understand them *in relation to the person of Jesus Christ.* That is a huge point, and one we'll pick up on later!

Luke 24

I've heard a lot of sermons in my life, and you probably have too! One sermon that I desperately wish I could have heard, however, is the one that Jesus "preached" to the two disciples, after his resurrection, on the road to Emmaus. You remember the story. Two followers of Jesus were walking along—going from Jerusalem to a town called Emmaus. Jesus had been crucified and buried just days before, and these two men were discouraged by the death of the man they had thought was the Messiah. All of a sudden, Jesus catches up with them and starts walking along beside them. But they don't know it's Jesus; "their eyes were kept from recognizing him" (Luke 24:16). As Jesus begins to ask the men about their conversation, they reveal that they're upset by Jesus' death. Jesus understands that they don't quite "get" it, so he begins to explain the meaning and purpose of his coming—his life, death, and resurrection. Here's how Luke briefly describes the explanation—or "sermon"—that Jesus gives these men: "And beginning with Moses and all the Prophets, he interpreted to them in all the Scriptures the things concerning himself" (Luke 24:27).

You see what I mean about wanting to hear that sermon? Jesus basically went through the entire Old Testament with those guys, and showed them how every single part—Law, Prophets, historical books, poetic passages, etc.—all related to *him!* What does this mean? It means that Jesus, as in John 5, is teaching his people to read and interpret the Bible with him at the center. As the climax. A right understanding of the entire Bible story *hinges* on grasping the fact that it's ultimately all about Jesus.

Sermons in Acts

While Jesus himself gives us some of the best and clearest statements about the centrality of his person to the story of the Bible, many other New Testament figures stress this fact as well. One great example of this is in the apostle Peter's sermon in Acts 2. Standing in Jerusalem, in the midst of Jewish people and leaders who know the Old Testament Scriptures, Peter argues clearly that the witness of the Scriptures ought to point them to Jesus' identity as God's Son—the promised King and Savior. Peter quotes from the prophet Joel, saying that the time of Jesus' coming is the fulfillment of all the promises recorded by the prophet (Acts 2:15–21). Then he quotes from a psalm of David, arguing for an interpretation of Psalm 16 that recognizes Jesus Christ as the ultimate "Holy One" of God. Here's what Peter says about King David's words:

> Brothers, I may say to you with confidence about the patriarch David that he both died and was buried, and his tomb is with us to this day. Being therefore a prophet, and knowing that God had sworn with an oath to him that he would set one of his descendants on his throne, he foresaw and spoke about the resurrection of the Christ, that he was not abandoned to Hades, nor did his flesh see corruption. This Jesus God raised up, and of that we all are witnesses. (Acts 2:29–32)

Peter is making the same argument that Jesus made in both Luke and John—that Scripture ultimately points to Christ. *All* Scripture points to him. Even the writings of David, Peter says, are ultimately about someone more than David. The psalms of David cannot be rightly understood until they are brought into their right relationship to the climax of the

Bible and the fulfillment of everything they speak about: the person of Jesus.

One Story with One Big Climax

So, we're making our way to the epicenter of the Bible's story. At the risk of sounding redundant, I'll say it one more time: the Bible is ultimately about Jesus Christ. He is the climax; the entire story draws its meaning from his life, death, and resurrection. And, like any other story with a dramatic climax, the various parts of the Bible's story cannot be rightly understood *until they are understood in relation to Jesus Christ.* Here's how one great scholar, Sidney Greidanus, describes this reality about the Bible: "Jesus Christ is the link between the Old Testament and the New. God's revelation reaches its climax in the New Testament—and this climax is not a new teaching or a new law, but a person, God's own Son."[2]

So the Bible has one big climax: Jesus Christ. He brings together the entire story. But what about the story itself? How does it develop? What are its various parts?

THE STORY OF THE KINGDOM

We have the most important part in place now: the Bible is all about Jesus. But there's obviously a lot to the Bible—sixty-six books' worth, to be exact! How do we describe the Bible's story, this story that has its climax in the person and work of God's Son?

Probably the clearest and best way to understand the Bible—and to "put the story together"—is by using the approach made famous by an Australian Bible scholar named Graeme Goldsworthy. Goldsworthy has suggested that the best way to understand the Bible is as the story of the *kingdom of God.* That concept is developed, and goes through much growth, from

Genesis to Revelation—it is a constant idea throughout the entire Bible. So, what is the "kingdom" of God? Goldsworthy describes it simply. The kingdom of God is always made up of three key elements: God's *people*, in God's *place*, under God's *rule*. We'll take a brief look at each of these elements, just to get an idea about how they develop throughout the Bible.

God's People

From the very beginning of the biblical story, we are introduced to a God who chooses to rule over—and be in relationship with—the people he has made. The concept of God's people expands and changes as the story of the Bible progresses, but God's people are always characterized by *God's saving and gracious actions toward them*. In the book of Genesis, we see God living in close relationship with his people, even speaking out loud to them, and giving them instructions for life in the garden of Eden (Gen. 2:16–17). After the fall, and the resulting expulsion from the garden, the sin of people in the world God has created becomes so heinous that, in Genesis 8, we see God's people whittled down to the family of one righteous man, Noah. God chooses to preserve these people from the flood that he uses to judge the world; he graciously gives them a covenant, and great promises.

In Genesis 12, we see a new development in the concept of God's people: God calls a man named Abram, and promises to bless him, and make from him a great nation and people for himself. This nation becomes the people of Israel, who grow and multiply, even during years of slavery in Egypt. Through Moses, God's chosen leader, God redeems and saves his people from slavery, and delivers them, in order to give them his law and bring them into the land he has for them. Throughout the historical books of the Old Testament, we see the growth of God's people—the Jews—and the formation of the monarchy and its centralization in Jerusalem. So, throughout the Old Testament, the concept of God's people is really focused on the Jewish people; God's saving and gracious work centers mainly on people who are *ethnically Jewish*. Still, there is that interesting phrase in God's call of Abram, the assertion that in him "all the families of the earth shall be blessed" (Gen. 12:3). This is an idea that the prophets pick up; Micah, for example, speaking to the people of Israel, looks forward to a day when "the mountain of the house of the LORD shall be established as the highest of the mountains, and it shall be lifted up above the hills; *and peoples shall flow to it, and many nations shall come*" (Micah 4:1–2). In other words, while the Jewish people are the focus of God's people in the Old Testament, there are these repeated indications that God's blessing, rule, and salvation are not only for people who are ethnically Jewish. This indication gets even brighter and clearer as the New Testament begins.

Jesus Christ—revealed by the gospel writers as the Messiah of God—is ethnically a Jew. He came first to the Jewish people, as he says many times (Matt. 15:24, for example). Yet the gospel narratives begin to reveal the truth that God's people—ultimately—are not identified first by their ethnicity, but by their faith and obedience, ultimately their faith in and obedience to the Messiah of God. Jesus speaks words of salvation to a Samaritan woman; he dines with Gentiles and "sinners." He angers the Jewish leaders by pointing to the faith of Old Testament Gentiles like the widow of Zarephath and Naaman the Syrian—two Gentiles who, by faith, were accepted as God's people (Luke 4:25–27). In other words, as the ministry of Jesus continues, we begin to see that God's people are ultimately identified not by their ethnic heritage, but by their response to Jesus, the Son of God. That is the very message, then, that the apostle Paul teaches in the epistles. There is no ultimate distinction between those who are Jewish and those who are

Gentiles. If entrance into the community of God's people comes through faith in Jesus, then God is "the God of Gentiles also" (Rom. 3:29). The fundamental belief about the continuity of the biblical story, then, is that the work, promises, and saving actions of God for the people of God—the Jews—in the Old Testament are ultimately applicable to the people of God—the church of Jesus Christ—in the New Testament and beyond. The identity of God's people has not changed; it has simply expanded. True "Israel" is now composed of all people who will receive Jesus Christ as King and Savior through repentance and faith.

We see this confirmed as we reach the end of the biblical narrative—the book of Revelation. God's people there are those who "have washed their robes and made them white in the blood of the Lamb" (Rev. 7:14). God's people, ultimately, are those who have responded to Jesus in faith and repentance, and have therefore received forgiveness and salvation through his blood. So the focus of who God's people are certainly expands and grows throughout the biblical narrative. But the key feature of God's people is the same from beginning to end: they are the recipients of *God's saving and gracious action*, which is fulfilled perfectly in Jesus.

God's Place

For Goldsworthy, a key component of the developing concept of God's kingdom is that his kingdom is a *place* for his people to dwell. This place is the *location for God's perfect rule over his people*. The first way this place is revealed to us in Scripture is, of course, as the garden of Eden. God puts the man, Adam, in this beautiful place "to work it and keep it" (Gen. 2:15). In this period it is a physical venue for God's people to live under God's rule. The rebellion and disobedience of Adam and Eve lead to their banishment from this good place.

After years of "displacement," and the scattering that occurs when the people try to build the Tower of Babel in Genesis 11, the prominence of place returns to God's relationship with his people in his call of Abram. As we discussed previously, this call includes the promise of the creation of a nation: a people. But there was also a promise of a place. God calls Abram with these words: "Go from your country and your kindred and your father's house to the *land* that I will show you" (Gen. 12:1). Part of God's call to Abram is a geographical transfer—a move to a place that God has both chosen and provided for his people. By the time of the Exodus account, however, this promise seems unfulfilled. God's people—the people of Israel—not only have no place of their own, but they are serving as slaves under the harsh leader of a foreign land.

The Exodus from Egypt—into the wilderness, but toward the land of promise—becomes a first step toward God putting his people in the place he has chosen and provided for them. It is Joshua, Moses' successor, who brings God's people into the land that God has for them. The book of Joshua records, first, the conquest of the land, and second, the division of the land among the people of God. It is a joyful and victorious account, as God's people receive a place to live under God's rule. It is in this place, then, the land of Israel, that the monarchy is eventually established with the city of Jerusalem as its capital. The palace of the king is there, as well as the temple, built by King Solomon.

But as God's people again rebel through idolatry, injustice, and rejecting God's Word, God judges them by giving their enemies victory over them. The exile—first for the northern kingdom of Israel, and then for the southern kingdom of Judah—takes God's people from their proper place. Even when the exiles eventually return, the place is never quite the same. The book of Ezra records how, when the temple was rebuilt after the exile, "many of the priests and Levites and heads of fathers' houses, old men who had seen the first house, wept with a loud voice" because they remembered the glory of the first temple (Ezra 3:12). By the time the New Testament begins, the people of God are back in their place, but under Roman rule.

In the New Testament, Jesus comes preaching a different and new message about God's place. Rather than calling an army to himself that will throw off Roman rule and reestablish the proper place of God's people in Jerusalem through political might, he affirms, "My kingdom is not of this world" (John 18:36). *Place* begins to take on a new meaning for God's people, as Jesus teaches his disciples about his "Father's house"—a heavenly house, with many rooms (John 14:2). The apostles, as they interpret the person, work, and ministry of Jesus to the early church, therefore have very little to say about a physical or geographical place for God's people. Their focus is on the "new heavens" and "new earth," which will come after the judgment of this world by Jesus Christ (2 Pet. 3:13). The Old Testament concept of God's place for his people—the promised land—becomes a picture of the heavenly home that God has always had in mind for his people: a perfect, eternal place.

Interestingly, the writer of Hebrews applies this heavenly focus on place even to the saints of the Old Testament. These saints were "seeking a homeland. If they had been thinking of that land from which they had gone out, they would have had opportunity to return. But as it is, they desire a better country, that is, a heavenly one" (Heb. 11:14–16). It is fitting, then, that the biblical story concludes climactically with the revelation of this glorious eternal place for God's people. The picture is of a city made for God's people, "coming down out of heaven from God" (Rev. 21:10). It is a picture, not just of part of creation, but of all the perfected heavens and earth, serving as the place for God to reign over his people with glory and joy. It is *the place where God's people will eternally dwell, living under the perfect rule of Christ the King.* It is the perfect and final home—the promised place—for the true people of God.

God's Rule

The foundation, or basis, of God's rule over his people is the fact that he is their Creator. The Genesis account makes it clear that God created human beings; we were God's idea! Compared to the developing concepts of *people* and *place* in the narrative of Scripture, the rule of God over his people is actually quite a simple concept, since God acts out this rule through one consistent feature: his Word. God, from Genesis to Revelation, *rules over his people by his Word.* We see this first, of course, in the book of Genesis. God creates the world, and human beings, by his spoken and powerful Word. He then gives instructions to the man he has made, for work (to keep the garden) and for obedience (to not eat of the Tree of the Knowledge of Good and Evil). The first person of God is, in this way, ruled by the Word of God as he lives in God's place; the fall results from the man and woman's failure and rebellious refusal to live under the rule of God's Word.

Abram, as he follows God's call for his life, also lives under the rule of God by means of the Word of God. God's call to Abram is for Abram to build his life on God's promises to him (the covenant). In short, Abram is ruled by God as he takes God at his Word. In Exodus and Leviticus, we see a broader revelation of God's Word as his means of ruling over his people. To the people God delivers from slavery in Egypt, he gives his Law—his authoritative Word of governance for how his redeemed people ought to live in relation to God and others (see Ex. 20 for the full context). The Israelites were thus a people of the Word; they were ruled by the spoken commandments of their God. Even under the divine establishment of the monarchy, the Word of God was meant to be the primary factor governing both the people and their king. Deuteronomy 17:18–20 makes this absolutely clear:

> And when he sits on the throne of his kingdom, he shall write for himself in a book a copy of this law, approved by the Levitical priests. And it shall be with him, and he shall read in it all the days of his life, that he may learn to fear the LORD his God by keeping all the words of this law and these statutes, and doing them, that his heart may not be lifted up above his brothers, and that he may not turn aside from the commandment, either to the right hand or to the left, so that he may continue long in his kingdom, he and his children, in Israel.

Even during the height of the monarchy, the primary ruler over God's people was not the king; it was to be God himself, through his authoritative Word for his people. It is precisely on this point that the prophets of the Old Testament make their appeal to a sinful and rebellious people. Their sin and idolatry is terrible not because it is a rejection of the human king, it is stunningly treacherous because it is a rejection of the Word of the living God. The Lord's words through Jeremiah demonstrate this: "Hear the words of this covenant and do them. For I solemnly warned your fathers when I brought them up out of the land of Egypt, warning them persistently, even to this day, saying, Obey my voice. Yet they did not obey or incline their ear" (Jer. 11:6–8). The broken covenant of God's people is their failure to accept the rule of God's Word over them; it is their failure to live under the rule God has always intended for his people.

The apostle John begins his gospel with a stunning declaration regarding the Word. He affirms that the Word of

God—Jesus Christ himself—"became flesh and dwelt among us" (John 1:14). In other words, the New Testament begins with the announcement that God's ultimate communication with his people, as well as his greatest mode of ruling over them, is wrapped up in the person of Jesus Christ, the Son of God. He is the Word "made flesh." He is the one to rule over God's people. However, as the New Testament progresses we see that the incarnate Jesus, the Word, does not rule out the necessity of God's written Word to lead, instruct, teach, and guide God's people. Paul commands Timothy to remain familiar with the writings of Scripture, because they are "able to make you wise for salvation through faith in Christ Jesus" (2 Tim. 3:15). Peter, even while recounting his eyewitness experience of the glory of Jesus the incarnate Word on the Mount of Transfiguration, identifies the scriptural prophecy and explanation of this event as even more sure than his own personal experience (2 Pet. 1:19).

In short, as the New Testament authors speak to us, we find that the written Word of God—the Scriptures that are inspired by the Holy Spirit—are actually the authoritative and necessary tool enabling God's people to interpret and rightly understand the death and resurrection of the incarnate Word! God's New Testament people are still to be ruled by the Word of God—Jesus Christ, as he is revealed to them through the Bible. The apostle John, as he closes the book of Revelation, therefore issues a warning: "I warn everyone who hears the words of the prophecy of this book: if anyone adds to them, God will add to him the plagues described in this book, and if anyone takes away from the words of the book of this prophecy, God will take away his share in the tree of life and in the holy city, which are described in this book" (Rev. 22:18–19). Until the day when God's people see Jesus, the incarnate Word, face to face in God's eternal place, they are to be ruled by God as he leads them through his Word.

ONE STORY IN BIBLE STUDY

OK. Take a deep breath. We've come a long way in this chapter. We started by discussing the fact that the Bible has a clear *climax* in the person and work of Jesus Christ, God's Son. Then we talked about the Bible as one connected story: the story of *God's kingdom* (God's people, in God's place, under God's rule).

This is so important, because the substance of this chapter is an important theological tool that will help you in the context of Bible study. We'll talk more about what a Bible study "tool" does later. But, for now, just stick with it! We need to lay this foundation. Students involved in Bible study need to carry this "one story" tool in their belts, preparing them to lead others in the study of any particular Bible passage in light of the big overall story.

In the next chapter, we'll dive into the implications of the unity of the Bible's story in a bit more detail. If the Bible is one big story about God's kingdom, climaxing in the person and work of Jesus, what does that mean for studying the various parts of the Bible? What about the psalms? The prophets? How do we make sure that we read *every* part of the Bible in relation to Jesus, while still understanding the details and meaning of each specific section, and their contribution to the developing pattern of God's kingdom?

DISCUSSION QUESTIONS

WHAT DID WE JUST READ?

1. What does it mean to say that the Bible is "one story?"

2. What are some ways that we know, from Scripture, that the Bible "hangs together" as one big story?

3. What are the different "parts" of the Bible's story? What is the climax?

4. What way does Graeme Goldsworthy suggest we can understand the developing story of the Bible? How is this helpful?

SO WHAT?

1. How does understanding the Bible as one story impact the way you study a particular passage?

2. How does understanding the climax—or main point—of the story shape how you look at every part of the story?

3. What can you do, in your personal or small group Bible study, to make sure that you're not missing the "big picture" of the Bible when you study individual parts?

7

STUDYING
THE BIBLE
AS ONE STORY

"To see the text in relation to Christ is to see it in its larger context, the context of God's purpose in revelation. We do not ignore the specific message of the text, nor will it do to write an all-purpose Christocentric sermon finale and tag it for weekly use . . . If you are tempted to think that most Old Testament texts do not present Christ, reflect on both the unity of Scripture and the fullness of Jesus Christ. Christ is present in the Bible as the Lord and as the Servant."
—EDMUND CLOWNEY[1]

HAVE YOU BEEN THERE?

Nick had recently studied Luke 24 with a few other guys, and the implications of what Jesus was saying were beginning to set in. As they studied the passage, they had been struck by verse 27: "And beginning with Moses and all the Prophets, he interpreted to them in all the Scriptures the things concerning himself." Nick and his friends had realized that Jesus' sermon was basically showing the two men who walked with him how the entire Old Testament pointed to him, and was ultimately about him. This was an amazing realization! It completely changed the way they looked at the stories, prophecies, and even poetry of the Old Testament. Nick and his friends were so excited that they decided to study a book of the Old Testament next. They knew a lot of the stories from 1 Samuel already, so they started with that. Before too long, though, they began to get a little "stuck." They understood the big picture: the Old Testament is ultimately about Jesus. But they didn't know quite what that meant for their study of a book like 1 Samuel. How should they "bring Jesus" into their discussion? How should they apply these passages as Christians following Jesus in the twenty-first century? Nick needed some help.

BIBLE STUDY IN ONE BIG STORY

So, if the Bible is one big story about God building his kingdom, climaxing in the life, death, and resurrection of Jesus, then what in the world does this mean for our Bible study? What difference should this make in the way we study, say, a passage in the book of Deuteronomy, or in 1 Kings, or in Revelation?

Implications for Study

We'll start by affirming an idea that we talked about back in chapter 5 when we were looking at Luke, John, and Acts—specifically, their argument for Jesus as the climax of the Bible. Here's the idea: you haven't really *gotten* a passage in the Bible until you've understood how it relates to Jesus Christ. He's the deal; he's the center of the story. So, if you don't understand how a passage relates to *him*, you're not done studying that passage in your Bible study! And there's a follow-up point: you can't get to Jesus from a passage without understanding that passage's place in the developing story of God's *kingdom*. That means we have our work cut out for us in Bible study. First, when we study any passage in the Bible, we'll need to figure out how it fits into the big story of the kingdom. Then, based on that, we'll need to figure out how it points us to Jesus, the kingdom story's central character. So . . . how do we do those things in Bible study?

Finding the Place in the Story

There is probably no more important activity in Bible study—at least initially—than this one: we've got to find our place in the big story of the Bible. Here are a few good questions to help us figure this out:

Where are we? The first thing we always need to do in Bible study is get properly situated. Imagine, for example, that you were randomly dropped into a car, speeding down a highway, somewhere in the United States. What would you need to do first? You'd probably need to figure out what highway you were on, find out what mile marker you were at, and then identify your location on a map! That's very similar to what we should be doing at any point in the story of the Bible. We need to pull out our "map" of the big story and find our place.

Think, for example, about studying the book of Judges in a small group. How do we situate ourselves, using the "map" of the Bible story? Well, first we remember where we've come from and what has happened so far. God's people have been set apart for God, and they have increased to a great number.

After a period of slavery in Egypt, they have been redeemed and freed by God's mighty hand. For many years they have wandered in the wilderness, but Joshua has finally brought them into the land God promised to them. So God's people are in God's place—the *land*. But there's a big problem in the book of Judges: God's *rule* is clearly not recognized by his people. The people are all doing whatever they want to do; there's no *king*! The book of Judges, then, is located at a key part of the story of the developing kingdom; it tells us that God's people need a king to rule over them, because they keep messing things up on their own.

What is God doing? This question is related to the one we've just discussed (finding our place in the story), but it's slightly different. We need to ask—at every point of the Bible story as we study it—what God is up to, as it relates to his people. Is God laying the groundwork for a monarchy for his people, as in the book of Judges? Is he establishing his people as a distinct people, as in the book of Genesis following the call of Abram? Is he showing his people the ultimate failure of a human monarchy and the need for a divine Messiah, as in the messages of many of the prophets? It will be incredibly important in Bible study to put our finger on what God is doing at a particular point in the history of his people.

What still needs to happen? The final question we should ask, in order to rightly "situate" ourselves in Bible study, is this one: "What still needs to happen in order for God's plan for the kingdom to be fully accomplished?" In other words, what are we waiting for? We'll approach this question from a slightly different angle in a moment, because it can't usually be answered without getting to a discussion about Jesus Christ, who is ultimately the centerpiece of God's great plan for his people.

The fact is, though, that every part of the Bible—whether it takes place before or after the coming of Jesus—implies that something still needs to happen. When we read the Old Testament, we do so knowing that Jesus' coming is expected, even demanded, by what is going on in any given narrative, psalm, or prophecy. When we study the New Testament, we do so knowing that the final chapter of the story hasn't happened yet; Jesus Christ still needs to return in glory to judge the world. A key aid to finding our place on the Bible "map," then, is asking ourselves what still needs to happen in the story.

Finding the Path to Jesus

Finding the path to Jesus in the story can be a little trickier than finding our place in the story. This is true, at least in part, because a lot of people "find" Jesus when he's not really there—at least not in the way they think he is! That's why I don't like asking the question "where is Jesus?" of every passage in the Old Testament. Technically, the correct answer for most Old Testament passages would be "nowhere." He hasn't shown up yet, at least not in his human form! The better way to think about this is in terms of the passage's *relation* to Jesus. Not "where is Jesus in this passage?" but "how does this particular part of the Bible relate to the climax of the Bible story?" I am not in any way suggesting that the entire Bible—including every part of the Old Testament—does not point explicitly to Jesus. It does; I will argue that in other parts of this book! The important point is to discover *how* every part of the Bible relates to Jesus.

Here are a few examples of the kinds of questions that can help to show how passages in Scripture relate to the central person and work of Jesus Christ, even if they don't mention him explicitly:

Does the passage directly foreshadow the work of Jesus? Some passages make it easy for us. Consider the account of the Passover, for example, in the book of Exodus. Exodus 12 lays out the story. God's people, enslaved to Pharaoh in Egypt, are about to be led out of the land by Moses, God's servant. Nine different plagues have already come down on Pharaoh and the Egyptians, and now it's time for the climactic, final plague, which will bring Pharaoh to his knees, so that he will finally let God's people go. Remember this awful plague? It's the death of every firstborn in the land of Egypt—"from the firstborn of Pharaoh who sits on his throne, even to the firstborn of the slave girl who is behind the handmill, and all the firstborn of the cattle" (Ex. 11:5). This devastating plague threatens even God's own people, but God gives them a *way out*. He gives them careful instructions that will cause them to be "passed over" when the angel of the Lord descends to bring death into the land of Egypt. What's the sign that God's people are to use? Blood. Specifically, the blood of a lamb without blemish, smeared on the doors of their homes. When the angel sees the blood, he will pass over their firstborn children and spare their lives.

It's not too hard to see that this account from the book of Exodus *directly foreshadows* the sacrificial work of Jesus Christ. In fact, all over the New Testament, Jesus is called the "Lamb" of God! He is the ultimate sacrifice for God's people—the ultimate "sign of blood" that allows God the Judge to "pass over" the sins of his people, and spare their lives. Now, that leads us to a key point in this discussion about paths to Jesus: a good indication of whether something in the Old Testament directly foreshadows the work of Jesus is *how the passage is used in the New Testament.* For the Passover story, it's an obvious fit; Jesus is actually referred to as the "Passover lamb" (1 Cor. 5:7). It is very clear that the New Testament writers (Paul, in this case) see the Passover event in Exodus as something that *directly foreshadows* the sacrificial death of Jesus Christ. That should guide and shape the way you lead a Bible study on Exodus 12!

Does the passage show us our need for Jesus? Some passages in the Old Testament are not so much like Exodus 12. They don't seem to directly foreshadow the person and work of Jesus Christ. So we have to ask a different kind of question. We need to see whether the passage—in some way—shows us *God's people's need for Jesus.* Some passages in the Old Testament are just dark; they don't seem to have much hope. That could be because they're there to show us that God's people need a Savior. In that case, they drive us forward to the coming of Jesus Christ, the great King and Savior of all God's people. Let's look at one example of how we might apply this question while studying the book of 2 Samuel.

In 2 Samuel 24, we find the account of King David's census of God's people. It's probably a passage that few of us have actually studied in a Bible study setting! We figure out pretty quickly that, while God is ultimately in control of the entire census situation, David's decision to number God's people in this way is a sin. It's a sign of pride; he's trusting in the size of his armies rather than in God first and foremost. So God is angry with David, and punishes the people of Israel for the sinful action of their king (2 Sam. 24:15). There doesn't seem to be much about this story that points us to Jesus, does there? How do we get there?

It seems that what a story like this does best is show us our *need* for a perfect king. The events of 2 Samuel 24 happen near the end of David's life. He's been—in a lot of ways—the greatest leader that God's people have ever had. And yet, even at the end of his life, he continues to fail in significant ways. *David is not the perfect and eternal King that God's people ultimately need.* Even King David falls short. At the end of David's life, we are left still looking forward to one who will come. A King who won't wrestle with personal pride, sin, and rebellion. A divine King. King Jesus.

Does the passage actually talk about Jesus? We've been talking mainly about Old Testament passages, because that's where it tends to be the hardest to find our way to Jesus in Bible studies. But, of course, a lot of your Bible studies will be in the New Testament. And a lot of New Testament passages (obviously!) talk explicitly about Jesus. For these, the Bible study question will be, what is this passage teaching us about Jesus? To put it a different way: What *specific contribution* is this passage making to our understanding of Jesus Christ? Some passages were written to clarify, for example, the results of Jesus' death on the cross. Some passages show us that Jesus is the great teacher of God's Word—the source of all wisdom. Some passages reveal that Jesus is the judge! It's important to discover what, specifically, the passage is saying about Jesus. Let's look at one example.

In the book of Philippians, Paul is calling the believers of the church in Philippi to have joyful unity together as they partner in the work of the gospel. Here's the appeal the apostle makes to them at the beginning of chapter 2:

> So if there is any encouragement in Christ, any comfort from love, any participation in the Spirit, any affection and sympathy, complete my joy by being of the same mind, having the same love, being in full accord and of one mind. Do nothing from rivalry or conceit, but in humility count others more significant than yourselves. Let each of you look not only to his own interests, but also to the interests of others. (vv.1–4)

Now Paul's going to bring Jesus Christ into the discussion. He's calling them to unity, remember, and telling them to humbly put others first. So, here comes Jesus:

> Have this mind among yourselves, which is yours in Christ Jesus, who, though he was in the form of God, did not count equality with God a thing to be grasped, but made himself nothing, taking the form of a servant, being born in the likeness of men. And being found in human form, he humbled himself by becoming obedient to the point of death, even death on a cross. (vv. 5–8)

What specific contribution is this passage making to our understanding of Jesus Christ, our Savior? Paul is showing us the *humble obedience* of Jesus, who went to the cross for the eternal good of others. Jesus is functioning, in this passage, primarily as an *example* for the people Paul addresses. Paul wants their attitudes and actions toward one another to be modeled after the attitudes and actions of Jesus. Does Paul spend time in other places in his letters talking about why Jesus died on the cross, and what his death accomplished for us? Absolutely! But that is not his focus here. In this passage, Paul is putting Jesus forward as an example. So, when we're studying Philippians 2 in a Bible study, that should be our focus too: Jesus, our example of humility and putting others first—the ultimate example, in fact.

CONCLUSION

So, the Bible is one big story. It's all about God's kingdom. That means, when we're studying any passage in Scripture, we've got to find our place in the big story . . . and we've got to ask the right questions to get there. The big story of the Bible has, as its climax, the person and work of Jesus Christ. That means, when we're studying any passage in Scripture, we've got to figure out how it relates to Jesus Christ, and we've got to ask the right questions to get there as well.

Well, if you're still reading that means you've made it through the most intense and theology-heavy part of this book. Congratulations! Just to review, we've made these points about the Bible:

- The Bible is **God speaking**—it is *inspired* by God
- The Bible is **powerful**—it has the *authority* of God behind it
- The Bible is **understandable**—it has *perspicuity* for us
- The Bible is **literary**—it has been *carefully crafted* by human writers
- The Bible is **one story**—it is *unified* around the person and work of Jesus

In the next chapter, we're going to try to work out a very clear definition of Bible study. We'll break it down piece by piece, and hopefully that will be helpful to you as you move forward in the various small group Bible studies you're involved in. Then we'll talk about some barriers that you'll face as you seek to study the Bible. After that, I'll give you some tools for studying the Bible in small groups—tools that have been very helpful to me. Let's move on!

DISCUSSION QUESTIONS

WHAT DID WE JUST READ?

1. What are some good questions to ask of an Old Testament text, in order to make sure that we understand where it "fits" in the story of the Bible?

2. What are some "safe" ways to determine how Jesus and the gospel relate to our passage?

3. How is the concept of "kingdom" helpful for studying the Bible as one big story?

SO WHAT?

1. How was this chapter helpful to you? How will you apply some of the "tools" and questions next time you study the Bible?

2. Why is it so important—as a Christian—to see how each passage in the Bible relates to the gospel?

3. What have been some of the hardest parts of the Bible for you to apply? Why is this? How can what you've learned from this chapter help you in future studies?

8

SO . . . WHAT *IS* BIBLE STUDY?

"You must remember this: You can never have a Christian mind without reading the Scriptures regularly because you cannot be profoundly influenced by that which you do not know. If you are filled with God's Word, your life can then be informed and directed by God—your domestic relationships, your child-rearing, your career, your ethical decisions, your interior moral life. The way to a Christian mind is through God's Word!"
—KENT HUGHES[1]

HAVE YOU BEEN THERE?

Hannah was frustrated. For a long time, she had wanted more out of her small group. The group, made up of Hannah and eight other teenage girls, met every single week. The girls liked each other—in fact they all got along very well. Every meeting started with a time for conversation and, usually, some kind of snack. Then they'd transition into a time of "study." Each week they focused on a different Bible passage. One person would read the passage . . . and then the part that frustrated Hannah so much would begin. The girls would make a few comments about what the passage was saying, but before long, one comment would trigger a tangential remark in a certain direction, and the girls would be off—speeding toward a (sometimes helpful) conversation about boys, movies, moral issues, or sharing the gospel with friends. A few times, Hannah had tried to voice her frustration to the group. "I really want this to be a *Bible study*," she'd said once. In response, the girls had affirmed that that was exactly what it was; they couldn't understand what was wrong with Hannah! Hannah wished she knew a clearer way to express what the group was missing—and what she was longing for. She wanted to dig into the Bible in a way that she felt they never did. How could she articulate what it was that she really wanted the group to accomplish?

WORKING TOWARD A DEFINITION

We've talked a lot about the Bible so far. And that's obviously where we need to start, if we're trying to get better at *Bible* study. What we'll try to do in this chapter, though, is work out a definition of Bible *study* that incorporates everything we've been talking about. In order to get to that definition, let's be clear about what good Bible study needs to include.

Trained Leaders

Good study of the Bible needs to be *led*, and those leaders need to be *trained*.

Now, am I saying that a group of people who have never read the Bible before couldn't pick up Bibles and get important truths about God, Jesus, and salvation out of their study? Absolutely not! That would go against our belief in the doctrine of perspicuity, remember? The Bible is understandable; the basic truths about God and salvation are "graspable" by anyone who reads it. But that doesn't mean that trained Bible study leaders aren't helpful—even *essential*—to small group Bible studies that are clear, effective, and profitable. So, what am I talking about when I say "trained" leaders?

What I'm not saying is that Bible studies have to be led by professionals! If pastors were the only people who could lead effective Bible studies, then our churches would be in a lot of trouble. Still, there is a certain amount of training in reading and understanding God's Word that will be absolutely necessary for every effective Bible study leader. What kind of training? Well, in short, training in everything we talked about in chapters 1 through 7 of this book. And it doesn't take a seminary degree to get this training! A small group Bible study leader, I believe, should have a good grasp of three things:

The storyline of the Bible. Now, this doesn't mean that a Bible study leader needs to be able to rattle off an outline for every book in the Bible; I certainly couldn't have done that when I was in high school or college! But it does mean that people who plan to lead a Bible study should have a decent grasp of the shape of the Bible's story. They should be able to, in their own words, sketch out the development of God's plan—in a similar way to how we did it back in chapter 6. Whether they use the "kingdom" language (God's people, in God's place, under God's rule) or talk about the covenant promises of God, they should be able to clearly tell someone—ideally in about five minutes—the story of God's redemption as it's revealed

147

to us in the Bible. At the least, their summary should include creation, the fall, God's promises to Abraham, the monarchy, the exile, the prophets, Jesus, the church, and heaven. Before you get too intimidated by what I'm saying, give it a try! Just try to describe the story of the Bible to a friend, giving yourself about five minutes. You may be further along than you think! Look back at chapter 6 if you need some reminders.

The message of the gospel. Any Bible study leader—from age nine to age ninety—should be able to clearly and succinctly express the gospel. There are different ways to explain the gospel, but the content needs to be there. The gospel is the "good news" that Jesus Christ, the Son of God, has fulfilled all God's promises to redeem his people from their sins, through his death on the cross and his resurrection from the dead. The apostle Paul puts it this way:

> Now I would remind you, brothers, of the gospel I preached to you. . . . For I delivered to you as of first importance what I also received: that Christ died for our sins in accordance with the Scriptures, that he was buried, that he was raised on the third day in accordance with the Scriptures. (1 Cor. 15:1, 3–4)

If the gospel—the work of Jesus Christ—is the central message of the Bible, to which we're supposed to connect every passage of Scripture that we study, then a Bible study leader had better be able to understand and clearly express the substance of the gospel! Again, it doesn't take a seminary education to get to that point.

The tools. It's possible to have a good grasp of the storyline of the Bible, and a good handle on the gospel, and still not do a very good job leading a Bible study in a small group setting. Some of you have experienced this, and you know how uncomfortable a poorly directed Bible study can be! Bible study leaders need to be equipped with the right *tools* to lead an effective discussion and study. That's what we'll get to in the next part of our growing definition of Bible study.

Asking the Right Questions

What makes a good Bible study? It's simple. It all comes down to *asking the right questions of the biblical text.* This is what separates a bad Bible study and a thriving small group discussion. It's also what sets Bible study apart from someone just standing up to give a sermon. Bible study involves a leader who knows how to lead the group in asking the right questions, so that together the group arrives at the meaning of the biblical text.

We'll leave this point here for now, because "asking the right questions" is essentially the topic of chapter 10. I'll give you several different methods—tools—that you can use in Bible study to make sure that you're asking the right questions of any passage in the Bible. When you finish this book, your Bible study "tool belt" should contain several reliable and effective approaches to asking these questions!

Hearing God's Voice

Bible study requires trained leaders who ask the right questions. That's where we are so far in our definition of Bible study. This last piece of the definition, though, is in some ways the most important part! It's what separates Bible study from a book club or a dinner party. It's what makes our study of the Bible different from our study of any other piece of literature in the world. It's what makes Bible study *actually worth doing.* Bible study, if it is truly Bible study, must emphasize *hearing God's voice*. That's why we study the Bible—to hear God speak! We began this book by making that point. Bible study should result in a group of people who go their separate ways having heard God speaking to them through the biblical text—and that should *make a difference in the way they live, think, and speak.*

You see, Bible study is not just a mental exercise, even though that's so often what we make it! Bible study that is done in the way God intended it to be done should be focused on, yes, getting the passage "right," but then *putting the passage to work in our lives.* In fact, the very reason we work so hard to understand God's Word accurately is so that we will come to better know our God, understand his ways, and live for Jesus, our Savior! Bible study that stops with a list of propositions about what a passage is saying has not done its job. The right study and understanding of God's Word must affect the way we live. God's Word needs to enter not only our heads, but also our hearts and lives.

> "Jesus had a small group, and it's a necessary part of a mature Christian's faith. Discussion about the Bible gives challenges to both the weak and the strong in faith; the weaker people see that they need to grow (and hopefully get inspired to get in the Word on their own) while the stronger people are shaken out of their complacency so they can ask questions and increase in wisdom. For myself, I need the fellowship and discussion in a small group because it pulls me out of my withdrawn, private faith enough to share this Christian life with others in a public faith. Whether you're an introvert or extrovert, we all need both."
>
> —Mike Solis (student, Wheaton College in Wheaton, Illinois)

THE DEFINITION

You've been waiting for my definition of Bible study, and here it is:

Bible study consists of trained leaders, asking the right questions, in order to help God's people hear God's voice in his Word.

Who leads Bible study? Leaders who are well trained in God's Word, so that they can guide a discussion skillfully. What happens in Bible study? A group of people ask the right questions about God's Word, so that they can rightly understand and apply it. What is the goal of Bible study? To help God's people understand his Word better, so that they can hear his voice clearly and live faithfully as followers of Jesus Christ in this world.

I hope you're already convinced that Bible study—defined this way—is worth doing! But I think it's important for us to acknowledge together that we face all kinds of barriers to Bible study today—especially as young people. So, in the next chapter, we'll discuss a few of those barriers.

DISCUSSION QUESTIONS

WHAT DID WE JUST READ?

1. What is the author's definition of Bible study? Does it make sense to you? Why or why not?

2. Why are the different parts of the definition of Bible study so important?

3. How do "Bible studies" that don't include one of the aspects discussed in this chapter sometimes fall short of their intended purpose?

SO WHAT?

1. How did this chapter change the way you think about Bible study?

2. What would you do differently, after reading this chapter, in your approach to studying the Bible in small groups?

3. How does the goal of Bible study make a difference in our attitudes and approach to it?

9

BARRIERS TO BIBLE STUDY FOR YOUNG PEOPLE

"It is apparent that most religiously affiliated U.S. teens are not particularly invested in espousing and upholding the beliefs of their faith traditions, or that their communities of faith are failing in attempts to educate their youth, or both. The net result, in any case, is that most religious teenagers' opinions and views—one can hardly call them worldviews—are vague, limited, and often quite at variance with the actual teachings of their own religion."

—CHRISTIAN SMITH and
MELINDA LUNDQUIST DENTON[1]

HAVE YOU BEEN THERE?

Tim, a thirty-year-old youth pastor, had just made a very difficult and painful decision. A seminary graduate, he loved God's Word, and was passionate about studying it personally and preaching it to the students he served. The Bible had come alive to him during his high school years, which was a major reason he felt specifically called to ministry with high school students. One of the first things he had done as youth pastor was to start several Bible studies with students from the group. He had put an older student in charge of each one, encouraged these leaders to invite their friends, and turned them loose. Tim was excited to see what would happen—he was optimistic that these groups would grow, and that his students would fall in love with the Bible together! That didn't happen, for several different reasons. Some groups complained to Tim: they wanted to spend more time "sharing" in their groups, and less time studying the Bible. Other groups told him, as gently as they could, that their leader just wasn't good at guiding the discussion. As the year went on the Bible studies began to dwindle. And that brings us back to Tim's decision: he had just made up his mind to end the Bible study groups, and do something different. As he wrote an e-mail to his student leaders informing them of this, he wondered where his plan had gone wrong. Had he missed something? Why hadn't the groups flourished? Why did it seem so hard for young people to study the Bible today?

OUR SITUATION TODAY

It's sad, but in most churches today good Bible study just isn't happening among young people. What I've seen—over and over again—is that gatherings that are labeled "Bible studies" don't actually get down to studying the Bible! They're excuses to get together and talk about feelings, problems, sin, and issues. (That's not all bad; we'll discuss the right place for these kinds of meetings later in this chapter.) In some churches, students have just stopped trying. They've abandoned Bible studies that were actually primarily about studying the Bible. Their small groups focus on something else, other than the study of God's Word. So, what are some of the major barriers to Bible study in the lives of young people today?

A Lack of Well-Trained Leaders

When Bible studies fail—or when they are abandoned altogether—you can bet that it's because their leaders have not been trained to lead Bible study well. Make no mistake: leading a Bible study is a *skill*. Some basic knowledge is required, as we discussed in the last chapter. Bible study leaders need to have a good grasp of the storyline of the Bible, the substance of the gospel message, and the tools to get to the heart of a biblical passage in a small-group setting. The sad thing is that very few churches are training their young people to lead others in the study of the Bible. I'm convinced that this should be one of the *first* things we commit to in youth ministry! We should be raising up students—young people—who are trained and equipped to lead others with skill and clarity in the study of God's Word.

If you're a teenager who loves Jesus and wants to know God's Word better, then you are capable of leading a Bible study! You'll need some training, but you can do it—I promise. So here's my challenge to you: find someone to train you. Talk to your youth pastor, another pastor at your church, or a mature Christian you respect. Tell this person you want to be trained to lead Bible studies of your peers. And get after it! If you're a youth leader reading this, you need to be training your student leaders to lead others in the study of God's Word. We'll talk more about how to do that in the next chapter.

"The challenging part is getting the students to connect the core message of a Bible passage directly to
their lives. So often students want to respond with a
surface-level answer or just regurgitate a response
that is safe. Students may not always like it when you
push back at them in searching for a true response,
but they need that. We first need to model this type of
reflection and application in our own lives as leaders.
Not only that, but we need to ask intentional questions. We need to help students see the deep heart
issues, sin, and struggles that the original hearers of
the Bible had, which should resonate so strongly with
our own situations. We must point them to the grace
within the passage that speaks directly to their life."

—Ben Panner (senior high pastor, College Church in Wheaton,
Illinois)

Bible Study Seems Boring

You've said this at some point, and so have I. We all have.
Why? Because sometimes it's true. Some of the Bible studies
I've attended have been really boring. But this is not the Bible's
fault, and it's not God's fault. You see, in reality, it's never boring
when God's voice is truly heard by God's people. Things get
scary, intense, beautiful, powerful, and convicting (sometimes
all at once) when God's people discern God's voice through
his Word. If Bible study is boring, it's not the Bible's fault. It's
our fault. It could be that the leader has failed to lead well;
he or she may not understand the passage, its relation to the
big story of the Bible, or its relation to the gospel. He or she
may have failed to engage others and help them ask the right
questions. Or it could be the group that has failed. They've
come to Bible study with a merely academic approach. They

haven't prayed that God will actually *speak to them* through his Word. That is a prayer that God delights to answer. And when he does, it's not boring!

Relevance Confusion

In my experience, young people often abandon Bible study not because they personally don't like it, but because they think it's not *relevant* to their peers. They just can't imagine that their friends would be interested in studying a book that is thousands of years old—and often hard to understand! So they try something different. They pick a topic to discuss. Or, to keep the Bible "involved," they use a verse of Scripture as a launching pad to a wider discussion about something that seems more interesting or relevant: sex, dating, friendship, whatever.

This attitude actually seems good at first, doesn't it? We want to reach our friends "where they are." We want to meet them with material and discussion that touches their lives in an immediately relevant way. A lot of you have done this out of good motives! You really want your friends to know Jesus better, so you try to find some way to make faith real to them. Here's the problem. When you lose focus on God's Word, you've lost the surest source of everything truly and eternally relevant to human life. You've entered, in other words, into relevance confusion. In your attempt to be more relevant, you've followed your agenda, rather than sticking to the Word of the God who created the entire universe—and all of us as well! When you give up an intense focus on the Word of God, you haven't become more relevant. You've actually *lost* ultimate relevance.

Let me put it a different way. If God really is the Creator of the world—including every man, woman, and child—then doesn't it make sense that in some way he would communicate to them *the most important things that they need to know about life, salvation, and himself*? God does do that! He does communicate to the people he has made! And he does it through his written and inspired Word—the Bible. That makes the Bible the most relevant thing we could ever read, study, or know. It contains the things that our Creator wants his people to know. That is real relevance.

Bible Study vs. Accountability, Prayer, Sharing, and So On

This barrier to Bible study is a big one. I've been in lots of small groups that have struggled to figure out this exact issue. Young people want to study the Bible, but they also want to share deep and personal struggles. They want to "get real" with each other by confessing sin, doubts, and emotional pain. They want to talk about the issues they face in school, and pray for each other as they live out their faith in a world that generally scoffs at the Christian call to holiness. Guess what? I want those things too. Every Christian should! We need a place to confess sin to one another—a place to talk, share our struggles, and pray for one another. You've probably noticed, though, the way those needs can "do battle" with a commitment to intentional Bible study—especially when you only meet for an hour. You just can't get it all done!

Let me suggest to you that one hour-long meeting simply *cannot accomplish all these things*. It is asking too much of any small group if we expect a weekly meeting to give us intense and substantive Bible study, real accountability and confession of sin, extended and rich prayer time, and vibrant fellowship and conversation with each other. There's no way you can do all that! Here's the solution: Bible studies should be Bible studies. We need a time—and a group—that is especially devoted to digging into the biblical text together, in order to know, understand, and apply God's Word better with each other's help. A Bible study should be about studying the Bible. Yes, prayer should be a part of it, but it's OK to end with just a few minutes of prayer after you've given the bulk of your time to digging into the Word.

I would suggest, then, having a *separate time* set aside for accountability, prayer, and confession with some close Christian friends. Ideally, this would happen in smaller groups that come out of a larger Bible study group (for instance, a Bible study of twelve people could split into three "quads" of four people each). These "smaller small groups" would meet at another time for intentional accountability, prayer, confession, and encouragement. We've done this with the men in our ministry, and it's given us a lot of clarity, both for our Bible study time and our accountability time! When you get together for a Bible study, *study the Bible.* Then, when you get together for accountability, you'll be able to give your complete attention to praying for one another, confessing sin and struggles (guided by God's Word, of course), and encouraging each other as brothers and sisters to press on as you follow Jesus together.

Our Beliefs about God's Word

Ultimately, the greatest barrier to a commitment to Bible study has to do with what we really believe about the Bible, doesn't it? If we really believe the Bible is what it claims to be—God's inspired, authoritative, powerful Word—then we'll be committed to studying it in order to know and understand it better. If we don't quite believe that, we won't. It really does come down to a conviction about God's Word.

So here's a question for you. Do you believe that Bible study is really *worth the work?* Is working hard with other people to know, understand, and apply God's Word really worth all the effort? Your answer will depend on what you believe about the Bible. If you know it to be the inspired communication of the God you love, worship, and know personally through Jesus Christ, your answer to those questions about the worth of studying it will be a resounding *yes*! On the other hand, if you find yourself unexcited and bored by the Bible, you may need to ask yourself some tough questions regarding your beliefs about the Bible . . . and your relationship with the God who inspired it.

CONCLUSION

There are certainly barriers to Bible study for young people; you know that as well as I do! But none of these barriers should get in the way of a vibrant excitement and commitment to know God's Word better. You—as a young person—need to break down these barriers. If you're not equipped to lead a Bible study, then find someone to train you. If you're trying to accomplish too many different things in your small group, then make the decision to focus on studying the Bible—and do your accountability and prayer another time. We all need to be studying the Bible. In the next chapter I'll suggest some specific tools you can use, as well as some general approaches for putting Bible study into practice.

DISCUSSION QUESTIONS

WHAT DID WE JUST READ?

1. What are a few of the "barriers" to Bible study for young people today that this chapter mentioned?

2. Can you think of any more potential barriers to Bible study, from your own experience?

3. According to the author, how can we begin breaking down some of these barriers?

SO WHAT?

1. How can you contribute, personally, to breaking down "barriers" to Bible study?

2. Is it true that a commitment to Bible study really comes down to our beliefs about God's Word? If you're honest with yourself, what are your beliefs, attitudes, and feelings about the Bible?

3. If you think that Bible study is really "worth it," how are you going to "go after it" with your peers and your church?

10

AIDS AND APPROACHES TO BIBLE STUDY

"The most immediate effect of sitting down to read a text is an encounter with a world that the text evokes in our mind, our awareness, our imagination. When we read, 'Once when Jacob was cooking stew' (Genesis 25:29, ESV), we are transported in our imagination to a time and place remote from our own. When Paul begins an epistle with the salutation, 'Paul, an apostle of Christ Jesus by the will of God, To the saints who are in Ephesus' (ESV), our minds and imaginations reach backward across the centuries to the first-century church at Ephesus, with its particular issues and concerns as these emerge from the unfolding epistle."
—LELAND RYKEN[1]

HAVE YOU BEEN THERE?

Chris was a senior at the large public high school in town. He had been involved in the youth group at his church for the past three years, but this year, his high school pastor had tapped him as a student leader. Over the summer Chris had met with the pastor once a week, training to lead a guys' Bible study though the youth group in the fall. They had gone over the storyline of the Bible; Chris had gotten a good grasp of how the "kingdom" theme developed throughout Scripture, and was feeling more and more comfortable jumping into any book in the Bible and knowing what was going on, and where he was in the story. He was also thrilled that—for the first time in his life—he could explain the gospel clearly, biblically, and confidently to his friends. He could even tell people how different parts of the Bible related to the gospel, and pointed to the life, death, and resurrection of Jesus. He was excited! Fall came, and eight guys gathered in Chris's basement to start Bible study. He had studied the passage for the past week; he felt that he could almost preach a sermon on it! Chris opened in prayer . . . and then realized he didn't know what to do next. What question should he start with? How would he get the guys talking about the passage? What tools could he use to help them discover *for themselves* the insights that he had already gained from the text?

NUTS AND BOLTS

In this chapter, we come down to the "nuts and bolts" of Bible study. Some of you are reading this and saying, "Finally! It's about time this guy started giving us some practical instructions about how to actually *do* Bible study!" If you're saying that, I understand where you're coming from. But please don't minimize the importance of everything we've gone through to get to this point. The theological principles that inform our understanding of and approach to God's Word lay the groundwork for any Bible study method you choose to use. Your *attitude* toward the Bible is the most important thing; the specific methods are secondary.

> "The continual pursuit of studying God's Word with students is one of the most rewarding experiences within ministry. Once a student falls in love with God's Word, then they are able to explode in their spiritual growth without the continual interaction with the youth leader. It is crucial for these students to learn context—the context of the passage of Scripture and the context which it fits into their normal lives. Students recognize that these letters, passages, and words were not always written to their direct circumstance, and they want to apply them the right way. The study of God's Word in the right context seems to change everything!"
>
> —Jeff Brooke (Bible teacher, Wheaton Academy in West Chicago, Illinois)

But the methods are important! Like Chris from the story above, many people know the Bible well and can study a passage for themselves, but they don't know how to *lead other people* to do the same thing. In other words, they need some "tools." That's what this chapter is about—filling your "tool belts" with tools that you can use when studying the Bible in small groups. All the tools that I'll mention here are good, so feel free to use any of them. Some are more helpful in specific situations and with specific kinds of Bible studies, and I'll point these out as we come to them. Here we go.

The Swedish Method

This is, by far, the easiest and most accessible method for studying a passage in the Bible. It's been used for years, and is a good way to get "beginners" into the biblical text. I've seen it work very well with students! Basically, there are three images that drive the discussion:

The lightbulb. As this picture suggests, you're looking for something that sticks out, or "shines," from the passage of Scripture you're studying. This could be something surprising, shocking, or extremely important. It could just be a confusing word or event that a new reader of the Bible gets hung up on. That's the beauty of starting with this picture: there are no wrong answers! You're just asking the group to identify things that "catch their eye" in the passage.

The question mark. At this point, the group identifies things in the passage that are hard to understand—things that raise questions in their minds. If anything was particularly confusing, troubling, or difficult, this is the place to bring that up. A good way to get at this discussion point is to ask the group, "If you could ask God one question about this passage, what would it be?" This gets them to engage with the text, and it's also a subtle reminder that, ultimately, it's God's Word that you're studying.

The arrow. This picture directs the conversation toward any personal application that the passage seems to call for. The group should be trying to discover what difference this passage was intended to make in people's lives. Some passages contain direct commands, so it's pretty easy to tell how to apply them. Other passages will make you work a little harder. You can ask questions like, "Does this passage seem to imply that

166

we should act or respond in a certain way?" or, "What lessons would God want us to learn from this passage about the way we live?"

The beauty of this method is that it's so simple, so memorable, and so accessible to people who have never studied the Bible before. It provides an instant "in" for them. And it's easy to lead, too! All you need is a piece of paper with three little pictures on it. You can even have a little fun with it, and bring in an actual lightbulb, a question mark on a piece of paper, and a toy bow and arrow. Here's the thing: even these simple pictures help people in a small group *focus on the text*. They help them begin asking questions, and working to discover what a passage in the Bible is saying to us today.

Observation/Interpretation/Application

Another very simple Bible study method is the observation/interpretation/application model. It's similar to the Swedish method, but a bit more focused in what it calls a group to do. This method is also a helpful one for people who are just beginning to study the Bible. It's easy to remember, and the three "sections" are clearly divided and defined. Here's how it works:

Observation. The basic question in this section is, "What do you *see*?" At this point, the group is focused only on making observations about the text. This is very similar to the lightbulb at the beginning of the Swedish method. Like that step, this section is helpful because there are really no wrong answers; anyone can make observations about a biblical text, even if it's the person's first time reading the Bible. The Bible study leader needs to be very intentional, during the observation section, to keep the discussion focused on *only* observation. Sometimes it can feel as if you're just stating the obvious—but this step is very important. You're making sure the group doesn't miss anything that's going on in the passage.

Interpretation. The next move, according to this method, is to begin interpreting the passage. First we asked, "What do you *see*?" Now we are asking, "What does it *mean*?" It's usually helpful to tackle parts of the passage bit by bit, working through the things that it is teaching and communicating. The goal in this section, though, is to settle—as a group—on the main point that the passage seems to be trying to get across. This can be a great group exercise; you're trying to summarize the "big picture" of the passage in one sentence. The Bible study leader should be helping the group put that sentence together, ironing out a simple and clear summary of the interpretation.

Application. Finally, the last step is to ask the question, "What does this mean for *us*?" Here the group moves on from mere interpretation, and begins talking about what difference the passage from God's Word should make in the way they think and live. This is a very important place for the group to get to, and it can easily lead into a time of prayer together that is very focused on the teaching of the Bible passage. The Bible study leader, in this step, should be guiding the group toward real, practical, and tangible applications of the passage. You can ask questions like, "What does that *really look like* in your life today?" or, "How should this affect your mind-set as you go about your day *tomorrow*?"

One benefit to leading a group using this three-step method is that the group will very quickly get used to the progression, and get better at working through the steps together. They'll have them memorized by the second week, and you can also encourage them to put those three steps to work in their own personal study of the Bible. A lot of Bible studies around the world are using this simple—but effective—tool for studying God's Word, and it can work very well, especially as the people who use it understand the "big story" understanding of the Bible, with the gospel as the center.

The "COMA" Method

This approach is very similar to the "observation/interpretation/application" method that we just discussed, so we won't spend much time on it. Here's what the acronym "COMA" stands for:

Context. The group spends time discussing the historical context of the Scripture passage (when, why, and to whom it was written), as well as the literary context of the passage (what came before it in the book, and what comes after it).

Observations. The group goes through exactly the same method described in the above section on observation—pointing out surprises, facts, and details that immediately "jump out" at them from the passage.

Meaning. This is the same thing as interpretation; the Bible study group moves toward the intended meaning—or "big idea"—of the passage. Together, the goal is to discover the main point that the authors intended to get across to their original audience—and to us today.

Application. Again, the goal is to begin to, as a group, apply the text directly to our lives. The group seeks to discover how the Bible passage should affect the way we live, think, speak, or believe.

The benefit of this method is the insertion of the "context" question, before diving right into observation and application. Again, this is pretty simple—but it works!

The Five Cs

This is a method that I adapted for our high school students from an approach that my college ministry used years ago.[2] My high school version seemed to work extremely well, particularly as we studied New Testament books. (The next tool I'll give you is the one we used for Old Testament books.) The Five Cs are five words, all starting with the letter "c," that guide the study of a New Testament passage. Here they are:

Creep. In the age of Facebook, my students are always using the word "creeping" to describe what they do to the Facebook pages of their friends—and what they don't want their parents doing to theirs! "You're such a Facebook creeper," I hear them say. So I've adapted that word to use it for a step in our Bible study, since they obviously know what it means!

Context. This word has a broad meaning; it's a reminder to look at the historical context of a passage in the Bible (when, why, and to whom it was written), but also the literary context (what comes before and after it in the book).

Christ. This is an obvious word, in some ways, but we are trying to get the students to do more than just put their finger on the place where Jesus *shows up* in the passage. We want them to ask the question, "How is Jesus presented to us in this passage?" In other words, we are trying to discover what *unique contribution* this passage makes to our understanding of Christ.

170

Crux. By the fourth C we are getting down to finding the main point the passage is making—the crux, or crucial part, of the passage. Sometimes, students identify a key verse that seems to wrap it all up. Sometimes they develop a general statement summarizing the main thrust of the passage.

Call. Every passage, I believe, contains a "call" for some kind of response. In this final step, we try to figure out what that call is, for our particular passage. This is the application part of the study.

Here's how I expanded each "C" question for our student leaders, to help them lead their Bible studies:

1. **Creep.** Creep on the passage (synonyms for "creep" include stalk, watch, observe, follow, etc.). Make observations. What words are repeated? What surprises you? What do you not understand? What does the tone seem to be? There is really no wrong answer here—just "stalk" the passage as closely as you can, and talk about what you observe!

2. **Context.** What is the historical context of the passage—who wrote it, why did the author write it, and to whom did the author write it? What is its literary context—what comes before and after it? What is its canonical context—what is its place in the Bible, and how does it relate to other parts of the Bible? Who are the characters mentioned in the passage?

3. **Christ.** If we believe that the Scriptures "bear witness" about Christ, then we ought to always be asking how any biblical passage fits in with the big story of God's redemption of sinners through Jesus, the promised Messiah. How does this passage illuminate God's plan? What do we learn about God? Is Jesus mentioned

171

explicitly? If so, what is he doing? What do we learn about him?

4. **Crux.** This refers to the crucial part of the passage—usually one verse that captures the key point the passage is making. If there is not one verse that you can identify as the "key," try your best in a short sentence to summarize the passage's "big idea."

5. **Call.** What does this passage call us to do? What is its application? Get real! Get specific! How should this passage make a difference in your life tomorrow?

The great thing about this method is that it is a little more "full" than the first two we discussed. It's ideal for people who are a little further along in their study of the Bible, because it calls for some discussion of context. But it's also very easy to remember, and it gives people a great tool to use both in group Bible study and on their own. In fact, at the end of the semester during which we used this method, one student approached me and said, "Jon, I'm so mad at you! I can't read any passage of the Bible now without thinking about those stupid 'Five Cs'!" I took that as a compliment.

The Five "Looks"

We developed this method in our youth ministry as well; it seemed to work especially well with Old Testament passages. Very simply, we were helping the students "look" in the right places in the passage, in order to get a good grasp of the narrative. Here they are, with some explanation:

Look at the passage. As do some of the other models we've covered, this one begins with observation. It's important to simply stop, look, and listen. You can ask questions like, "What jumps out at you when you read this passage?" or,

"What surprised you when you read this for the first time?" This question also gives the group a good opportunity to get absolutely clear about what's actually happening in the story. Let's face it—sometimes Old Testament stories use culturally specific terms, or refer to events or practices that are just hard for us to understand today! We want to look at the passage closely to make sure we actually understand what is going on.

*Look at the **people**.* In Old Testament passages, we need to begin by focusing on the people in the narrative. What are they doing? What are they learning? What mistakes have they made? How are they responding to God—either negatively or positively? The more we see and understand the behavior of the people involved in the story, the more we can prepare to appropriately apply the Bible passage to our lives today. This question also gives the group a chance to talk about the main characters of the story, which we all know is an important part of understanding a plot!

*Look at **God**.* As a Bible study leader moves the group toward this third "look," it's important to issue the reminder that we, as Christians today, serve and follow the same God who sovereignly ruled his people in the Old Testament. Some significant changes have occurred, yes, because Jesus has come. But God's perfect character has *not* changed. So it's important to focus specifically on what every Old Testament passage is teaching us about God. You might ask, "What are we learning about God's *character* in this passage?" or, "What were the people *in this story* being taught about God?" or even, "Does God do or say anything in this passage that was *surprising* to you?" In any passage in Scripture, a safe question to ask is, "What is this passage teaching us about *God*?"

*Look to the **gospel***. We've already talked about the fact that not every passage in the Old Testament specifically foreshadows Jesus. Still, the fact that the message of the gospel is the central point of the Bible forces us to ask how every passage in the Bible *relates* to that gospel message. At this stage, the group leader should be trying to help the group look at the Old Testament passage *in light of Jesus' death, resurrection, and eternal rule*. Some questions you might ask are, "Does this passage show us, in a powerful way, humanity's need for a final solution to sin?" or, "How does this passage hint that God will need to act in a drastic way to save his people?" Sometimes, of course, Jesus will be directly foreshadowed in a passage; some stories just beg for us to point them forward to him! Many, though, will take some work, as well as an understanding of how the whole story of God's salvation unfolds, and is completed and perfected in his son.

*Look at your **life***. The last "look" asks us to begin to apply the passage to our lives directly. The call is to look at our lives and ask, "What difference should the truths of this passage make in the way I think, act, believe, and live?" Some passages call us to change the way we think—about God, for example. We may be called to remember that God is infinitely holy, or that he judges sin. Other passages seem to call for a more active response: we must, as followers of God, forgive others, or give generously to those in need. The group leader, in the process of this "look," should be helping the group see how the passage should make a tangible difference in the way Christians live. The goal is to connect the teaching of the passage to our lives *right now*.

Genre-Specific Discussion Questions

All the approaches to Bible study that we've discussed so far are very helpful—and also very simple. They have the benefit of being easy to remember. They're "catchy," and a group can quickly get into the rhythm of studying passages using the Swedish Method or the Five Cs. This last tool is the most advanced, and also the least "memorable." This method is probably best used by people who have fairly significant experience studying the Bible.

The goal here is to use—or write (for very experienced and well-trained Bible study leaders)—Bible study discussion questions that are specifically geared toward the *genre* of Scripture that you're studying. We're talking about six different sets of questions here: questions designed for narrative, prophecy, wisdom/poetry, apocalyptic writing, gospel, and epistle. Probably the best practice for this is to have a team of Bible study leaders compose these questions together (we'll talk more about this team approach in the next chapter). Here are some examples, though, to give you an idea what these genre-specific questions might look like:

Narrative.
- What is the shape of this narrative's plotline? Who are the characters, and what are they doing?
- Where are we in the storyline of the Bible? What are God's people immediately hoping for in the context of this passage?
- What do we learn about God in this passage from his actions, presence, or words? How is he the hero of this story?
- What do we learn about human beings from this passage? How are they supposed to respond to God?
- How does this passage point us forward to Jesus—or the need for Jesus?

Prophecy.
- What was the historical situation for God's people during the ministry of this prophet? How does it

cast light on what the prophet is talking about in this passage?

- How is this prophet showing us the character or actions of God? How is God presented to his people in this passage?
- What would you say is the prophet's tone in this passage? Is he talking about judgment, hope, restoration, or something else?
- What response was this passage designed to provoke in the lives of its original hearers? What response should we have today?
- How does the life, death, and resurrection of Jesus Christ shed light on the meaning of this passage?

Wisdom/poetry.

- What is the main point of this passage? Is there a repeated phrase, word, or theme that you can see? Does a specific situation seem to have prompted its writing?
- How does the writer use images, examples, metaphors, or vivid language to communicate?
- How is this passage designed to present God to us? What do we learn about him from this passage?
- Is there a specific call or instruction to God's people in this passage? If not, does the passage seem to imply a certain response to God or his Word?
- How do you, as a follower of Jesus, apply this passage? How does it help, encourage, or challenge you today?

Apocalyptic writing.

- What is the mood or tone of this passage? How are the words and images intended to make you feel?
- What seems to be the "big picture" of what is going on in this passage? Is it a scene of judgment, salvation, peace, destruction, or something else?

176

- Where is God, and what is he doing?
- What are the people doing? How are they responding to God, and how is God relating to them?
- How might this passage be pointing us to Jesus? What role does he play in the lives of God's people, in relation to this passage?

Gospel.
- What is going on in the story? Who are the main characters, and what do they do?
- What is Jesus doing? What does he seem to be trying to accomplish or teach?
- How do the characters in the story respond to Jesus?
- What, specifically, does this passage contribute to our understanding of Jesus? What does the gospel writer seem to focus on, concerning his life, teaching, or ministry?
- How are we being called, by this passage, to respond to Jesus?

Epistle.
- How does our knowledge of the author and recipients of this letter help us understand what is going on in this passage?
- What came just before this passage? What will the author go on to discuss after this passage? How does this context help us understand the passage?
- What, specifically, is the writer of this letter trying to help us understand about God, or Jesus Christ?
- Is the author calling for a specific response from his readers, either implicitly or explicitly?
- How should we apply this passage as Christians today?

These genre-specific questions could certainly be tweaked! But they give you a sense of how the questions can vary quite a bit, if you want to go into a little more detail in any given genre. Still, you can also probably see that, using one of the simpler models, you'd eventually find your way (with the help of a good leader) to the same basic understanding and application of any given passage.

CONCLUSION

So you've got some tools! I encourage you to take this chapter and put it in your metaphorical "tool belt" for Bible study. Try these methods; see what works and what doesn't work in your specific context. The important thing, remember, is helping the group ask the right questions. If you do that, you'll usually find your way to the meaning—and the right application—of any passage in the Bible. Use your tools!

In the next chapter, we're going to take a slightly broader look, not just at methods, but at *approaches* to Bible study. How do we actually *train* leaders? How can Bible study leaders encourage, challenge, and help each other lead?

DISCUSSION QUESTIONS

WHAT DID WE JUST READ?

1. What is one method of Bible study that this chapter mentioned?

2. Have you used any of these methods before? If you've used more than one, which one do you think was most helpful?

3. How are some methods better for certain kinds of groups than others? Give one example.

SO WHAT?

1. How would using a set method—or "tool"—for Bible study be helpful in your small group context?
2. If you were going to start a small group Bible study with your friends today, which method would you choose? Why?
3. What is the ultimate goal of any of these methods? What are they all trying to help people accomplish as they study the Bible?

11

LEADING TOGETHER

"We need a different mental picture of church life and pastoral ministry—one in which the prayerful speaking of the word is central, and in which Christians are trained and equipped to minister God's Word to others. Our congregations become centres of training where people are trained and taught to be disciples of Christ who, in turn, seek to make other disciples."

—COLIN MARSHALL and TONY PAYNE[1]

HAVE YOU BEEN THERE?

It was April, and Rachel was already starting to think about graduation, which was only a couple of months away. It had been a great senior year—filled with sports, friends, school events, and, of course, college applications! Rachel had also enjoyed the year in her high school youth group at church, where she had served as one of the core student

181

leaders. She and nine other seniors had met once a month with the youth pastor and his wife, and had talked a lot about the youth ministry. They had had great discussions, and had spent a lot of time praying for the youth ministry and for the hearts and lives of troubled students in the church. Rachel's youth pastor had done a great job involving the student leaders in planning and vision-casting for the year; they had felt that they were really part of the "team." The students had even planned a big outreach night all by themselves. And yet—Rachel couldn't shake a feeling that, although she had been a student leader, she hadn't really learned much or developed her skills as a Christian leader, teacher, and discipler. She'd been involved in events, meetings, and prayer, but she didn't feel that she was walking away from the experience any more equipped to lead in the church in significant ways. She wondered if the same thing would happen when she joined a church during college . . .

WHAT IS STUDENT LEADERSHIP?

Every youth ministry that I've observed or been part of has had some kind of student leadership team in place. I've seen these teams, which are usually made up of older students, do everything from lead music to buy food to plan events. Almost always, these student leaders love Jesus, care about the hearts and souls of their peers, and want to make a difference for the growth of the gospel in their churches, schools, and towns. Yet my guess is that many of the student leaders in our churches today move on from their youth groups feeling a bit like Rachel. They've had a fun time . . . but are they *equipped* to do ministry on their own now? More specifically, have they been *trained to handle God's Word well* during their years in student leadership?

FROM EVENTS TO EQUIPPING

A Needed Shift

What I want to suggest to you—as a student, or as a youth leader—is that we make a major shift in the way we think about the role of "student leadership" in our churches. I want to suggest a move from *involving student leaders* to *training student ministers.* By "ministers," I don't mean pastors! I mean students who speak, teach, and spread God's Word in a significant way. In other words, I would like to see us shift from teaching our students to run *events* to intentionally *equipping* our students to handle God's Word and communicate it clearly to their peers. And I'd like to suggest that the best way to do this is to train them to lead effective and vibrant small group Bible studies.

Before we talk more specifically about what this looks like, let me clarify what I'm saying here. I'm *not* saying that having student leaders help run events, plan retreats, or lead music is bad. Those are, of course, good activities, and it's wonderful to have students take ownership of them while they are still students! But if this is all we do, we haven't equipped our students with some of the most important skills we can give them—skills that relate directly to studying, understanding, and communicating God's Word.

Potential Approaches

With this "shift" in mind, here are a couple of specific approaches you might consider:

Change your student leadership team into a student training team. This doesn't have to change the role student leaders play in retreats, events, games, or music! What it should change is the focus. According to this model, student leaders are primarily students who are intentionally *trained* by the youth leader. Student leaders should come away from their time on the leadership team with an ability to clearly articulate the gospel. They should be able to give a clear overview of the storyline of the Bible. They should have several "tools" in their pocket to lead Bible studies of their peers—at church or at school. They can still lead the youth group in significant ways. But they will also go away better equipped to be ministers of God's Word to the people around them.

> "I believe that students desire to be challenged. I believe we can push students toward thinking deeper and harder about their faith. In Bible studies with students, we must train students to study the Bible themselves. Students find it boring when adult leaders sit and talk the whole time, giving students the 'answers.' One of the most exciting things to see as a youth leader is students reading and discussing passages of the Bible together, finding the essential message of a passage on their own. Students enjoy that challenge of finding the truth themselves. Granted, students will need guidance in this process, but they can be trained to look on their own."
>
> Ben Panner (senior high pastor, College Church in Wheaton, Ilinois)

You'll find that there are many benefits to this model. One is that it opens the leadership team to students who are not "natural leaders," but who love Jesus and love God's Word. These students need to be trained as well! They may not be the outgoing, passionate, and vibrant up-front leaders, but many of them are more than capable of leading a small group

Bible study with a handful of other students. Some of them may actually be *better* in that context than their peers who tend to grab all the attention at youth group. This training approach can also take some of the mystique out of the student leader "thing." You're not necessarily setting up a group of "super-spiritual" student leaders who are going to be perfect examples to their peers! You're selecting a team of Christian young men and women who want to be trained to be more effective ministers of the gospel.

Do "live" Bible study together in your team meetings. You obviously need to have some meetings just for planning events. There are retreats to organize, youth nights to arrange, and strategies to discuss. But the best thing that a leadership team—at any level of the church—can do is *study God's Word together.* So, if you're studying the gospel of John in your small groups, and you have student leaders leading the small groups, then set aside a good portion of your leadership meeting to *study the gospel of John together!* There is no better way to equip and train students to lead Bible study than to show them how it's done. Pick a tool that you'll use throughout the year, and then do "live" Bible study together in your team meetings. Go through the questions together. Don't "fake" it—really study the Bible together. Pray. Apply the text. There's no better way to get ready to lead others in the same thing!

We made this shift in our youth ministry, for both our student leadership and adult leadership meetings. We realized that we could take care of a lot of the logistics and details of the ministry in phone calls and e-mails over the course of the week. So we decided to change the focus of our monthly meetings, and use those times to study together the passages of Scripture that our small groups would study during the coming month. With both the adults and the students, my goal was to model the role of a small group Bible study leader. I asked the questions, led them through the study, and guided the discussion. From time to time, I'd stop to give some specific directions about leading the discussion. But, in general, we were doing "live" Bible study. I think our team was strengthened through this, and our Bible studies got better and richer, because our goal was to prepare and train for them.

Make "student leader" synonymous with "small group leader." Part of the problem with the student leadership teams in many youth ministries is that, far too often, no one really knows what it actually means to be a student leader! Sometimes, "student leader" becomes merely a title—a vague description that fits neatly into the "Church/Community Involvement" section of a high school student's application for the National Honor Society. My suggestion is this: student leaders should be *small group Bible study leaders.* This should be, if not the only aspect of their leadership role, at least a core part of it. Why?

A small group Bible study gives students a real place in which to learn to lead. More than this, it gives them a smaller, "safer" venue than in a big group meeting in which they can learn to speak and teach God's Word more effectively, clearly, and powerfully. This is different from just showing up on a youth group night and trying to "play the part" of a student leader. Small groups give students defined roles; they are called to help lead their peers to look together at God's Word, discuss it, and apply it to their lives.

This model also prepares students to begin to "shepherd" other believers in a genuine way. Even if a lot of the students in the group are the same age as the student leader, there's still a shepherding kind of activity that happens through the leadership of a small group. There's really no better venue in which to learn to speak and teach the Word effectively and lead others in a real way than a small group setting.

CONCLUSION

I realize that some of the things I'm arguing for would demand a major shift in the way many churches engage in youth ministry. But I want to ask again this important question: What kind of students do we want to be sending out from our churches? Or, to put it a different way, what tools do we want our students to have as a result of serving as student leaders in their youth groups at church? There is *no greater gift* that we can give our young people than the necessary training to read, understand, and apply the Bible—and the tools to help other people do the same! That's the vision behind this model. It's a conviction that, more than anything else, we want to help our young people engage with Scripture, and in so doing, become equipped to lead others to engage with it as well.

DISCUSSION QUESTIONS

WHAT DID WE JUST READ?

1. What are some of the major "shifts" that the author suggests for the way we view student leaders in youth ministry?

2. What ultimate goal are these changes designed to achieve?

3. Why, according to the author, is Bible study a perfect place for training younger Christians?

SO WHAT?

1. If some of the changes described in this chapter actually happened in your youth ministry, how would that affect the student leaders?

2. Personally, would you be excited about some of the "shifts" that this chapter describes? Why or why not?

3. If studying God's Word is really so important, are there other "shifts" you can think of that might need to occur in our churches and youth ministries?

12

A CALL TO
YOUNG PEOPLE

"I . . . tell students (only partly in jest) that the three
most important rules for interpreting the Bible are:
(1) Read it. (2) Read it again. (3) Read it again."
—WAYNE GRUDEM[1]

HAVE YOU BEEN THERE?

Jessica had been a Christian for as long as she could remember. She had grown up in the church, and in a family that loved God's Word; they read from the Bible every night after dinner, in fact! Now a sophomore in high school, Jessica was consistent—if not perfect—in her daily devotions. She tried to read and study Scripture every morning before school, and she spent time in prayer as well, seeking to apply each passage to her life. As she'd grown in her love for the Bible and her understanding of its power, authority, and sufficiency, though, she'd become increasingly restless and uneasy with the youth

189

ministry at her church. Her youth pastor obviously loved the Word; he usually preached messages that were grounded in one passage of Scripture, and he paid careful attention to the text. But Jessica was realizing that—aside from these messages—her experience in youth group had not involved much Bible *study*. Small groups were places to talk, hang out, pray, and share—but there wasn't really much careful study of the biblical text. There certainly wasn't a focus on *training* the students in the ministry to read and study God's Word. Jessica knew something needed to change. She loved her church, her youth group, and her pastor—but she craved a deeper study of God's Word that could happen alongside her peers in small group settings. She decided to talk to her youth pastor about this desire . . .

A CALL TO BIBLE STUDY

As we get closer to the end of this book, I pray and hope that you've learned more about God's Word along the way. I hope you've been encouraged to consider the power, authority, and inspiration of the Bible—and that those realities forever shape the way you read it, study it, and teach it. More specifically, I hope you've formed a conviction, along the way, that people who love Jesus and love God's Word *must* do Bible study! So, in this final, brief chapter, I want to *call you to engage in Bible study*. To really get going. To dig into God's Word. In other words, you may agree in your mind with everything this book has been about—but you'll demonstrate that belief by actually committing yourself to studying the Bible with your peers.

So, here's my call to you: *commit yourself to studying the Bible in small groups*! I have several grounds for issuing this call, and I ask you to consider them very carefully and thoughtfully.

Rather than writing out, in paragraph form, an extended explanation of why you should "go after" Bible study, I've decided to put before you eight reasons that I hope will be pretty compelling. That is, they'll be compelling if you do love Jesus and love God's Word! Why should you go after Bible study? You should go after it for your (1) holiness, (2) relationship with God, (3) training, (4) witness, (5) mind, (6) leadership, (7) church, and (8) friends. I'll explain briefly what I mean by each of these reasons for this call.

"Students in our culture are constantly fed the lies that they are basically good ('trust your heart, and do what feels right'), yet that they are essentially worthless. Only from God's Word do students find security, fulfillment, and hope. They find it when they come to understand from God's Word that they are fallen and depraved, and that their heart is desperately sick. They find it when they come to understand why they need forgiveness and that it has in fact been offered. They find it when they come to understand and believe that the Creator-God of the universe chose them to be purchased out of sin at the cost of his perfect Son's death on a cross because of his love for them. They find value, worth, and love as the adopted children of God through Jesus Christ. Only God's word can undo the lies being powerfully propagated."

—Jason Draper (lead pastor, Harvest Bible Chapel in Dekalb, Illinois)

Study the Bible for Your Holiness

One surprising way that Scripture talks about itself has to do with the sanctification of believers in Jesus Christ. Sanctification—the process of being made more holy and like Jesus by the power of the Holy Spirit—is often, in Scripture, closely associated with the work and influence of God's *Word*. Listen to Jesus' prayer for his disciples in the book of John: "Sanctify them in the truth; your word is truth" (John 17:17). Jesus' prayer to God for the sanctification of his disciples very obviously involves the influence of the Word of God in their lives. God's Word is connected to our growth in holiness. In other words, we're not going to become more like Jesus, our Savior, without the influence of the Bible in our lives!

The apostle Paul talks about this same reality in his letter to the church at Thessalonica: "God chose you as the firstfruits to be saved, through sanctification in the Spirit and belief in the truth" (2 Thess. 2:13). What does the experience of salvation look like for a believer in Jesus Christ, according to Paul? It involves sanctification in the Spirit *and* belief in the truth (which we know is found, ultimately, in God's Word). Growth in holiness happens by the power of the Holy Spirit, who dwells in us through faith in Jesus Christ. But this doesn't happen in some mysterious way that is disconnected from the influence and working of God's Word in our lives! We grow in holiness as we understand and apply the Bible more and more to our hearts and lives.

The call to study the Bible—specifically in small groups—is an earnest plea to take your sanctification *seriously*. If becoming more like your Savior is intricately connected to the impact of the Bible on your life, then you should be taking every opportunity to know and understand the Bible more and more! That means you sit under good biblical preaching, of course. It means you read the Bible devotionally, like Jessica in the story that began this chapter. But it also means you study the Scripture carefully with brothers and sisters in Christ. When you do that, you're not just performing a mental exercise or going to a church-based book club. You're pursuing your own sanctification, as you allow God's Holy Spirit to work in your life through the witness of God's Word.

Study the Bible for Your Relationship with God

Really, the strongest—and simplest—reason to call you to Bible study should be your personal relationship with the God of the Bible. On what basis should Christians dig into God's Word? On the basis of their *love* for the God who has so graciously communicated to them! A love for God, in other words, should imply a love for the Bible—his Word. If you find yourself with absolutely no desire to study and know God's Word better, then it may be time to ask yourself some questions about your relationship with God.

To put this in a slightly different way, we see throughout Scripture that people who love God always love his Word as well. It's impossible to have a love for God and a hatred for his Word (or even an apathetic attitude toward it). One place we see this connection of love between God and his Word is in Psalm 119—an extended "love song" about God's Word. Just listen to one part of this psalm:

Oh how I love your law!
    It is my meditation all the day.
Your commandment makes me wiser than my enemies,
    for it is ever with me.
I have more understanding than all my teachers,
    for your testimonies are my meditation.
I understand more than the aged,
    for I keep your precepts.
I hold back my feet from every evil way,
    in order to keep your word.
I do not turn aside from your rules,
    for you have taught me.

How sweet are your words to my taste,
   sweeter than honey to my mouth!
Through your precepts I get understanding;
   therefore I hate every false way. (Ps. 119:97–104)

Let me ask you a question: Is *that* the way you feel about the Bible? Now, I'm not saying that every single morning when you wake up to do your devotions you'll be singing with ecstatic joy and enthusiasm. But it does seem clear that God's true people really do love, value, and cherish his Word. At the very least, this love ought to bear fruit in the way we *put systems in place* in our lives to help us know the Bible better. That's the argument for biblical preaching, personal devotions, and yes, small group Bible studies!

Study the Bible for Your Training

The call to Bible study is for your sanctification. It's the natural result of your love for your God. But it's also a call for your *training* as a follower of Jesus Christ! Every Christian—headed toward full-time ministry or otherwise—is under the same "big" call of Jesus Christ. Here's that call, in the words of Jesus himself:

> And Jesus came and said to them, "All authority in heaven and on earth has been given to me. Go therefore and make disciples of all nations, baptizing them in the name of the Father and of the Son and of the Holy Spirit, teaching them to observe all that I have commanded you. And behold, I am with you always, to the end of the age." (Matt. 28:18–20)

We are all called to be disciples of Jesus Christ, which implies committing ourselves to "making" more disciples of Jesus Christ! What is the best way to do this? To be *trained to better understand and communicate God's Word*. The best context—

at least at the outset—for this kind of training to happen is in Bible studies. Leaders who are trained and equipped to lead discussion (in the right way) become more familiar with the gospel, the storyline of the Bible, the methods and approaches to studying Scripture, and even the best ways to lead a group of people to an understanding of God's Word. What better way to be trained to make disciples of others? A commitment to Bible study that is done well implies a commitment to training disciple-makers.

Study the Bible for Your Witness

This point is related to the last one, but takes a slightly different focus. A commitment to Bible study—for you personally—can and should help you serve as a faithful witness to others of the gospel of Jesus Christ. Far too many youth groups and churches are filled with people who *receive* good gospel preaching week after week, but are never actually trained and equipped to effectively bear witness about that gospel, which they do genuinely believe and love. A commitment to Bible study can be a perfect way to prepare students to bear witness about the good news of Jesus Christ to the people around them. Why is this the case?

First, it's the case because—in the process of Bible study—questions come up. Big questions. Important questions. Questions about each specific passage, that relate to the major theological themes of the entire Bible! A commitment to Bible study is a commitment to wrestle through the witness of Scripture with other people. When you do that faithfully, you'll find that you're more and more equipped to respond clearly and faithfully (and biblically!) to the difficult questions that unbelievers are asking about God, Jesus, and the Christian faith. Why? Because you've wrestled with those questions in various texts of Scripture!

195

Second, Bible study can serve as a faithful and effective witness of the gospel because there is no better way to tell people about God's salvation than to *invite them to read and study the Bible with you.* There are certainly good "plans" and approaches for sharing the gospel with people. But, if we really believe the Bible is all that we've been saying it is, then the absolute *best* way to bring someone to Jesus is to let the Bible do the work. It's to let God speak to people through his Word! Bible study prepares you to help other people ask the right questions of God's Word—and discover his truth through it.

Study the Bible for Your Mind

In 1 Peter, the apostle writes this to a group of early Christians who are spread out around Asia Minor: "Therefore, preparing your minds for action, and being sober-minded, set your hope fully on the grace that will be brought to you at the revelation of Jesus Christ" (1 Pet. 1:13). Peter's call to them, obviously, is to set their hope on Jesus Christ, and ultimately on his future appearing to complete their salvation. But what's really interesting are the participle phrases Peter chooses to use to modify the imperative "set your hope." They both have to do with our *minds.* Christians should "prepare" their minds for action. Literally, this phrase carries the sense of wrapping our garments up around our legs to prepare for some kind of strenuous activity. That is the way we need to get our minds ready to engage with a world that has, largely, rejected the gospel of Jesus Christ. This mental engagement will be strenuous activity, and we need to get ready for it! The second phrase Peter uses—"being sober-minded"—probably refers to the practice of seeing reality accurately. It is a call to see the world the way God sees it.

How does a Christian do these things? How do we both "prepare" our minds and remain always "sober-minded" as we hope in Jesus Christ? Friends, there is only one way to do those things. It's by *actively giving ourselves to the study and knowledge of God's Word, the Bible.* How can we best prepare our minds for battle? By knowing God's Word, and all its truth, extremely well. How can we think rightly about reality? By learning to think about the things of this world in biblical categories. This means thinking about our world like God thinks about our world; we learn that kind of thinking from immersing ourselves in Scripture. The best way to prepare our minds, and to learn to think rightly about reality, is to study and know the Bible—personally and in small groups!

Study the Bible for Your Leadership

I've become more and more convinced that the ability to lead, facilitate, and guide a small group discussion—particularly in the context of Bible study—is an incredibly valuable skill. And it's a skill that a lot of people who can preach and teach very effectively simply don't have! At its core, leading and guiding a small group study is all about leadership skills. You have to *listen* to people, in order to truly understand what they mean, and why they're saying what they're saying. You have to have a clear *goal* in mind for the study, so that you can provide both direction and guidance to shape the discussion. Finally, you have to help the group *discover for themselves* the truths of the Bible passage that you're studying together. This is the most difficult part by far! It's what separates Bible study from classroom lectures and Sunday sermons. But, when this actually happens, it's incredibly rewarding. You get to see someone actually figure out how to do Bible study. That is so much better than just giving them the "right answer" about a passage.

Ultimately, I believe that what I've just described is a hugely important part of being a good leader in any context. Listening to people, guiding them toward a goal, helping them make discoveries on their own—all of those are valuable skills for politicians, doctors, lawyers, pastors, coaches, and businesspeople.

Study the Bible for Your Church

Why should you "go after" Bible study? You should do it for the sake of your church! Let me explain. You will be a *better and more effective member of your church* if you commit yourself to knowing, understanding, and applying God's Word well—no matter what age you are! You'll be able to begin contributing to the life of your church in genuine ways. At one time or another you may have heard someone talk about approaching the Bible in a "Berean" way. Here's the passage where that comes from; it's in the book of Acts. Listen to the description of the Berean people:

> The brothers immediately sent Paul and Silas away by night to Berea, and when they arrived they went into the Jewish synagogue. Now these Jews were more noble than those in Thessalonica; they received the word with all eagerness, examining the Scriptures daily to see if these things were so. (Acts 17:10–11)

It's through a commitment to Bible study that you can begin to engage with the teaching and preaching of your church more like these "noble" Bereans. You'll listen more carefully to preaching, both to apply it to your life and to test the words of the preacher against the words of Scripture. The goal is not to constantly be "checking up" on your pastor, but there is a sense in which *you are personally responsible* to make sure that you're being taught biblical truth, and not just the opinions of a human being. Friends, your church will be *better* if this is true of you. In fact, every church will be stronger the more it is filled with people who search the Scriptures carefully—both on their own and in the context of regular, careful, intentional Bible study with others.

Study the Bible for Your Friends

You should begin studying the Bible in groups for the sake of your *friends*. That is what I'm saying here! If it is really true that the Bible is the best thing for us as Christians, then what does it mean to be a true Christian friend? At least it involves, at some level, helping our friends understand, know, and apply the Bible better and better. If I believe, personally, that the reason I study the Bible is to hear God speak to me—an activity that is intricately connected with my growth in holiness—and I don't help my friends "get there" as well . . . I'm a big hypocrite. And I'm not truly loving my friends in a Christian way!

A commitment to studying the Bible in small groups is a commitment to *helping your friends grow in their faith, understanding, and relationship with God.* That's what makes Bible study in small groups such a valuable activity! You are sharing your wisdom and insights (yes, we all have these, to some extent!) with other people, to their spiritual benefit. In other words, your friends need you. They will grow as they work together *with you* to know God's Word more fully. I'm calling you to commit yourself to Bible study with the spiritual benefit of your friends in mind.

GO FOR IT!

You've heard the call: go after Bible study! My prayer is that the study of God's Word will become a central part of your personal walk with Christ and your relationships with God's people. If you give yourself to diligent Bible study, I know that you will be blessed by the riches of Scripture. That will be good for your heart and soul—and good for the people you lead!

DISCUSSION QUESTIONS

WHAT DID WE JUST READ?

1. How is the Bible linked to our sanctification, according to this chapter? Does this change your attitude toward Scripture?

2. Why is Bible study an effective way to both "train" young people and prepare them to "witness" to others about Jesus?

3. Ultimately, what does this chapter argue that a commitment to Bible study really hinges on?

SO WHAT?

1. In light of this book, have you been convicted about your attitude toward God's Word? If so, in what way?

2. Are you studying the Bible regularly? Why or why not? How can you grow in this area of your Christian walk?

3. What are some ways that you can encourage your peers to study the Bible? How can you be a leader in this area?

CONCLUSION

Moving Forward—
A Different Scene

"How do we receive the Word of God? By use of the faculties that God has given us: our ability to read, hear, reason, feel. But of course, our sin makes it impossible for us to use these capacities rightly apart from his grace. What keeps us from suppressing the truth . . . is the Holy Spirit, who opens our eyes to perceive the full blessing of God's address to us and who enables us to rejoice in God's kindness. . . . So we can understand God's revelation only through the gospel. In that sense Scripture, the message of the gospel, takes primacy over all of God's revelation. It becomes the 'spectacles' (John Calvin) by which we are enabled to see God's revelation in creation rightly."
—JOHN FRAME[1]

SIX HIGH SCHOOL STUDENTS sit together in a family room, somewhere in the Midwest. They're doing a Bible study together. Ben, the discussion leader, asks the guys and girls to open their Bibles to Philippians 4:10–13, their passage for the evening. As they settle into the couches and chairs on which they are sitting, Kristen reads the passage out loud:

> I rejoiced in the Lord greatly that now at length you have revived your concern for me. You were indeed concerned for me, but you had no opportunity. Not that I am speaking of being in need, for I have learned in whatever situation I am to be content. I know how to be brought low, and I know how to abound. In any and every circumstance, I have learned the secret of facing plenty and hunger, abundance and need. I can do all things through him who strengthens me.

Ben begins by calling the group's attention to the most well-known verse in their passage—verse 13. "What are some places you've seen that verse displayed?" Michael, a football player at the local Christian high school, jumps in: "We've got that verse pasted right over the bench press in our weight room. I guess it's supposed to inspire us to lift more weight!" Hannah mentions an experience at a Christian summer camp, where she and the other campers were instructed to yell out, "Philippians four-thirteen!" as the boat pulling them on water skis prepared to speed up.[2] "So," Ben asks, "in what *way* is that verse being used in those instances?" Different people begin chiming in, and the general consensus of the group is that—in the context of weight room and water skis—Philippians 4:13 is being used to inspire Christians toward greater *accomplishment*.

Ben then turns the conversation toward some questions he's prepared to help them study the passage together. The first one has to do with context. "Where is Paul, when he writes this letter?" he asks. The group quickly remembers and agrees that Paul most likely wrote the book of Philippians from a Roman prison. "OK, that's the historical context," summarizes Ben. "Now, in the immediate context of this letter, what is Paul talking about *before* verse 13 of our passage?" The group looks back at the text, and Hannah reads verses 10 to 12 aloud one more time. It's Michael, the football player, who finally summarizes well what the entire group is realizing: "Paul's not really talking about *accomplishment* here, he's talking about *contentment*." The conversation continues, and together the group moves toward a fuller understanding of this passage from Philippians. They spend some time in prayer, asking God together that—in every situation—they would have contentment, knowing that Jesus Christ is their ultimate source of strength, joy, and peace.

Kevin hasn't said much. He found out earlier in the day that he has been cut from the football team. On top of that, he is really worried about his AP History class, which he knows will be a big challenge for him academically. He doesn't feel very confident about being able to "do all things" in any area of his life right now! But, as he begins to understand what the apostle Paul is talking about, Kevin begins to hear God speaking to him through his Word. As the Bible study goes on, God's voice is quietly telling him that he can be *content*; in Christ his Savior, he can do "all things"—even if that means finding joy in Christ in the midst of disappointment, stress, or pain. Kevin walks away encouraged. The apostle Paul went through suffering, prison, loss, and rejection, and his Savior was *enough* for him to remain content. Kevin knows that same Savior, and he reminds himself that Jesus really is enough for him.

EPILOGUE

A Word to Pastors and Youth Directors

BIBLE STUDY ISN'T JUST GOING TO magically get easier
overnight. In our college ministry today, we are still trying to
get better at studying God's Word in groups, and I don't think
we have by any means mastered all the skills or perfected our
use of all the "tools." Still, we believe that it is valuable, so
we're sticking with it. We're continually tweaking our methods
and approaches, but holding onto the conviction that God's
people need to be trained and equipped to study God's Word
on their own—and lead others to do the same.

Here is my core belief on this point: a youth ministry,
college ministry, or local church ministry will thrive and
grow (in the right ways) as the ordinary members are taught,
trained, and equipped to study God's Word on their own.
The best Bible expositors cannot—merely through preaching—help people do this. We need to commit to intentionally training our people to study the Bible on their own,
and in small groups. This is something that pastors need
to *decide* to "get after"; it won't just happen naturally. If we
want to equip and train our people to understand God's

Word, teach it, and lead others to study it in small group settings, then we need to put resources, time, and people into this cause.

If you're a youth pastor or teaching pastor, let me urge you to understand that this kind of a commitment will only *bolster* and *enhance* your teaching and preaching ministry. If you really give yourself to training and equipping your people to study God's Word in groups, you'll find that—over time— you will have a congregation that listens to and engages with biblical preaching with more hunger, more discernment, and more passion. You'll find that you are more and more challenged by them; hopefully you're not intimidated by that! This is by no means a commitment that competes with your leadership or your preaching; it should only encourage your ministry, and allow you to preach to people who are more apt to hear the Word, and more eager to apply it to their lives in the right ways.

Let me make one final appeal to you on this point. We (pastors) need to be training our *women* to understand God's Word, teach it, and lead others in Bible study. I am complementarian in my view on the roles of women in the church, because I'm convinced by Scripture that the role of pastor/elder is reserved for men only. But that does not mean that there is not *significant Word work* that our women need to be "turned loose" in our churches to do! Far too often, those leading churches within the complementarian camp allow women's ministries to become filled with "fluff"—high on relationships, and low on rich, deep, *biblical* content. When this happens, you can be sure that there is little training happening! The best gift we can give to the women in our congregations is to help them handle the Bible well. We need to help them interpret and apply it on their own, and we need to give them tools to lead other women

206

in Bible study and rich Bible teaching. This is a task that is *not* reserved for men only!

I do pray that this book has been helpful for you, your youth ministries, and the parents and families of your church. By God's grace, I pray that in the coming years we will see more and more local church congregations that are filled with networks of genuine Bible study, especially among our young people. For, after all, we want them to hear *God* speak.

NOTES

Introduction

1. Christian Smith and Melinda Lundquist Denton, *Soul Searching: The Religious and Spiritual Lives of American Teenagers* (New York: Oxford University Press, 2005), 134.

Chapter One: The Bible Is God Speaking

1. D. A. Carson, *Collected Writings on Scripture* (Wheaton, IL: Crossway Books, 2010), 19.

Chapter Two: The Bible Is Powerful

1. Philip Ryken, "Preaching That Reforms," chap. 12 in *Preach the Word: Essays on Expository Preaching: In Honor of R. Kent Hughes*, ed. Leland Ryken and Todd Wilson (Wheaton, IL: Crossway Books, 2007), 197.

Chapter Three: The Bible Is Understandable

1. Wayne Grudem (quoting Deut. 6:6–7), "Right and Wrong Interpretation of the Bible: Some Suggestions for Pastors and Bible Teachers," chap. 4 in Ryken and Wilson, *Preach the Word*, 57.

2. John M. Frame, *The Doctrine of the Word of God*, A Theology of Lordship 4 (Phillipsburg, NJ: P&R, 2010), 207.

3. Grudem, "Right and Wrong Interpretation," 57.

Chapter Four: The Bible Is a Literary Work

1. Kathleen Buswell Nielson, *Bible Study: Following the Ways of the Word* (Phillipsburg, NJ: P&R, 2011), 60.

209

2. Leland Ryken, *The Word of God in English* (Wheaton, IL: Crossway Books, 2002), 159–160.

3. Ibid., 158–159.

4. Ibid., 159; quoting C. S. Lewis, *Reflections on the Psalms* (New York: Harcourt, Brace, and World, 1958), 3.

Chapter Five: Exploring Biblical Genres

1. Dennis E. Johnson, *Him We Proclaim: Preaching Christ from All the Scriptures* (Phillipsburg, NJ: P&R, 2007), 273.

2. Vaughan Roberts, "Preaching from OT Narrative," Charles Simeon Trust Preaching Workshop, Wheaton, IL, 2012.

3. We'll discuss this concept more in chapter 6, "The Bible Is One Story."

4. Wayne Grudem, *The Gift of Prophecy in the New Testament and Today* (Wheaton, IL: Crossway Books, 2000), 21–22.

Chapter Six: The Bible Is One Story

1. D. A. Carson, *Collected Writings on Scripture* (Wheaton, IL: Crossway Books, 2010), 19.

2. Sidney Greidanus, *Preaching Christ from the Old Testament: A Contemporary Hermeneutical Method* (Grand Rapids, MI: Eerdmans, 1999), 49.

Chapter Seven: Studying the Bible as One Story

1. Edmund P. Clowney, *Preaching Christ in All of Scripture* (Wheaton, IL: Crossway Books, 2003), 11.

Chapter Eight: So . . . What *Is* Bible Study?

1. R. Kent Hughes, *Disciplines of a Godly Man* (Wheaton IL: Crossway Books, 2001), 77.

Chapter Nine: Barriers to Bible Study for Young People

1. Christian Smith and Melinda Lundquist Denton, *Soul Searching: The Religious and Spiritual Lives of American Teenagers* (New York: Oxford University Press, 2005), 134.

Chapter Ten: Aids and Approaches to Bible Study

1. Leland Ryken, *The Word of God in English* (Wheaton, IL: Crossway Books, 2002), 151.

2. The college ministry at College Church in Wheaton, Illinois, led by Randy Gruendyke, used a method similar to this one.

Chapter Eleven: Leading Together

1. Colin Marshall and Tony Payne, *The Trellis and the Vine: The Ministry Mind-Shift That Changes Everything* (Kingsford, Australia: Matthias Media, 2009), 99.

Chapter Twelve: A Call to Young People

1. Wayne Grudem, "Right and Wrong Interpretation of the Bible: Some Suggestions for Pastors and Bible Teachers," chap. 4 in *Preach the Word: Essays on Expository Preaching: In Honor of R. Kent Hughes*, ed. Leland Ryken and Todd Wilson (Wheaton, IL: Crossway Books, 2007), 55.

Conclusion

1. John M. Frame, *The Doctrine of the Word of God*, A Theology of Lordship 4 (Phillipsburg, NJ: P&R, 2010), 291.

2. This is a true story! One of our students told me how this happened at a summer camp. The campers were supposed to use that reference as a reminder that they could "do all things" through Christ—even get up for the first time on water skis!

BIBLIOGRAPHY

Carson, D. A. *Collected Writings on Scripture*. Wheaton, IL: Crossway Books, 2010.

Clowney, Edmund P. *Preaching Christ in All of Scripture*. Wheaton, IL: Crossway Books, 2003.

Douglas, J. D., ed. *The New International Dictionary of the Christian Church*. Grand Rapids, MI: Zondervan, 1978.

Frame, John M. *The Doctrine of the Word of God*. A Theology of Lordship 4. Phillipsburg, NJ: P&R, 2010.

Greidanus, Sidney. *Preaching Christ from the Old Testament: A Contemporary Hermeneutical Method*. Grand Rapids, MI: Eerdmans, 1999.

Grudem, Wayne. *The Gift of Prophecy in the New Testament and Today*. Wheaton, IL: Crossway Books, 2000.

Hughes, R. Kent. *Disciplines of a Godly Man*. Wheaton, IL: Crossway Books, 2001.

Johnson, Dennis E. *Him We Proclaim: Preaching Christ from All the Scriptures*. Phillipsburg, NJ: P&R, 2007.

Marshall, Colin, and Tony Payne. *The Trellis and the Vine: The Ministry Mind-Shift That Changes Everything*. Kingsford, Australia: Matthias Media, 2009.

Nielson, Kathleen Buswell. *Bible Study: Following the Ways of the Word*. Phillipsburg, NJ: P&R, 2011.

Roberts, Vaughan. "Preaching from OT Narrative." Charles Simeon Trust Preaching Workshop, Wheaton, IL, 2012.

Ryken, Leland. *The Word of God in English*. Wheaton, IL: Crossway Books, 2002.

Ryken, Leland, and Todd Wilson, eds. *Preach the Word: Essays on Expository Preaching: In Honor of R. Kent Hughes.* Wheaton, IL: Crossway Books, 2007.

Smith, Christian, and Melinda Lundquist Denton. *Soul Searching: The Religious and Spiritual Lives of American Teenagers.* New York: Oxford University Press, 2005.

"From his years of counseling experience, Lou Priolo has developed a work that exposes many of the prideful manifestations of people-pleasing, while also walking the reader through the biblical process of repentance from the heart. This is a book that God can use greatly to change lives."

—**Stuart Scott,** associate professor of biblical counseling, the Southern Baptist Theological Seminary

"Even if you think you do not have this weakness, you may be convicted that you do! The strengths of this book are its biblical principles, its charts with wrong compared to right ways of thinking, and its counsel on how to become a 'God pleaser.' I am very pleased to have this resource for helping people."

—**Martha Peace,** author of *The Excellent Wife* and *Damsels in Distress*

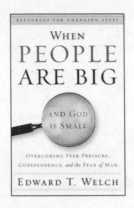

"Need people less. Love people more. That's the author's challenge. . . . He's talking about a tendency to hold other people in awe, to be controlled and mastered by them, to depend on them for what God alone can give. . . . [Welch] proposes an antidote: the fear of God . . . the believer's response to God's power, majesty and not least his mercy."
—*Dallas Morning News*

"Refreshingly biblical . . . brimming with helpful, readable, practical insight."
—**John MacArthur,** president of The Master's College and Seminary

"Ed Welch is a good physician of the soul. This book is enlightening, convicting, and encouraging. I highly recommend it."
—**Jerry Bridges,** author of *Trusting God*

Popular culture plays a huge role in our day-to-day lives, often influencing the way we think and see the world. Some people respond by trying to pull away from it altogether, and some accept it without question as a blessing.

But Ted Turnau reminds us that the issue is not so black-and-white. Popular culture, like any other facet of society, is a messy mixture of both grace *and* idolatry, and it deserves our serious attention and discernment. Learn how to approach popular culture wisely, separating its gems of grace from its temptations toward idolatry, and practice some *pop*ologetics to be an influence of your own.

"Ted Turnau does a great service toward helping Christians engage their culture with both conviction and open-mindedness . . . and offers excellent practical application for how to both appreciate pop culture and fairly critique it."

    —Brian Godawa, Hollywood screenwriter, author of *Hollywood Worldviews*

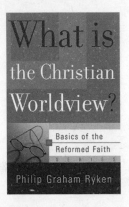

What does Christianity have to do with ordinary life? Is there a biblical perspective on our work or recreation or whatever we do? If so, how can we gain that perspective?

Many people seek to have a biblical view of life, yet fail to apply that biblical mindset, or worldview, to all parts of their lives. Ryken reveals the basis of the Christian worldview and describes how it affects one's view of God, creation, the family, work, the arts, and other issues.

Basics of the Faith booklets introduce readers to basic Reformed doctrine and practice. On issues of church government and practice they reflect that framework—otherwise they are suitable for all church situations.

OTHER BOOKLETS IN THE SERIES INCLUDE:

The heart is the source of all human motivation. Our hearts contain motives such as pleasure, happiness, meaning, power, comfort, control, success, peace, freedom, reputation, respect, and love/intimacy. Welch encourages us to ask questions to discover some of our deeper motives: What do you hope for, want, crave? What do you fear? What do you worry about? When do you say, "If only . . ."?

OTHER BOOKLETS IN THE SERIES INCLUDE:

Anger, David Powlison
Depression, Edward T. Welch
God's Love, David Powlison
Homosexuality, Edward T. Welch
Just One More, Edward T. Welch
Pornography, David Powlison
Suicide, Jeffrey S. Black
Thankfulness, Susan Lutz
Why Me?, David Powlison

"The gospel isn't just an ethereal idea. It's not a philosophy and it's not static. It moves and shapes and transforms the lives of those who by God's grace alone put their faith in Jesus' life, death, and resurrection. I am grateful for [the Association of Biblical Counselors]'s work of letting the gospel bear its weight on these real life sorrows and pains."

—**Matt Chandler,** lead pastor, The Village Church

ALSO IN THE SERIES:

Abuse, John Henderson
Anxiety, Robert W. Kellemen
Borderline Personality, Cathy Wiseman
Burnout, Brad Hambrick
Depression, Margaret Ashmore
God's Attributes, Brad Hambrick
Post-Traumatic Stress Disorder, Jeremy Lelek
Sexual Abuse, Robert W. Kelleman
Vulnerability, Brad Hambrick

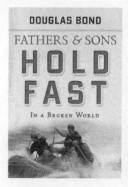

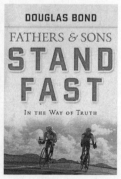

Fathers & Sons is a two-volume set of 48 readings. The books allow over a year of close fellowship between father and son, with the goal of leading sons toward Christian manhood. Taking serious issues seriously, yet promoting a joyful life of enjoying the pleasures of God, these books show that the stakes are high when a young man makes decisions about the direction his life will take.

"Full of lively illustrations, wise warnings, and hard-hitting application for everyday life, Bond's latest book addresses all of the strong temptations and difficult trials that young men face today."
  —**Philip Graham Ryken,** president of Wheaton College

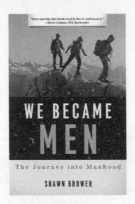

Life is a journey—a journey of adventure, discovery, risk, and revelation. This book is a guide that affirms and validates young men and empowers them to pursue manhood from a biblical perspective. It will give you clear vision and direction for your life in vital, life-changing areas such as performance, temptations, relationships, idols, boredom with life, and much more.

"Don't just buy this book; read it, live it, and teach it!"
  —**Steve Connor,** NFL linebacker

"Young men, if you are up for a challenge, read this book! Brower challenges us to step up and take *responsibility*—for our hearts, souls, and lives—under the authority of God's Word. This is a great read for young men who are seeking to live truly (and biblically) masculine lives in service to the Lord Jesus Christ."
  —**Jon Nielson,** Pastor for Senior High, College Church, Wheaton

Also by Shawn Brower: *The Huddle: Becoming a Champion at Life*